D1447355

M.K.
Planting Heaven

M.K.
Planting Heaven

Soosung Her
&
Ellen Eun Her

Published by Ellen Her Foundation
Design by YKBooks Inc. in Korea
Printed in Korea(Pandacom Inc.)

Soosung Her & Ellen Eun Her

M.K. Planting Heaven

Ellen Her Foundation
35 Sparrowhawk,Irvine,CA 92604
(718) 509 9078 / (949) 351 5020
tccofhs@yahoo.com

ISBN / 978-1-5323-9932-9

To Ellen

Even though you are no longer with us,

I leave these words as a memory of my lovely daughter,

who is now planted as a seed of the Kingdom of God on this earth.

Foreword

A heartfelt congratulations on a book that has reached beyond just a Korean speaking audience to an English-speaking audience.

This comes from the heart of a missionary couple who experienced a great tragedy in burying their young child on the mission field. This book can be said as recounting written on the paper of sorrow, by the pen of faith, and with the ink of hope. All those who would approach this book with an open heart will witness the powerful encounter of time and eternity, as well as the meeting of heaven and earth.

The main character and co-author of the book, Ellen, when she was in the 3rd grade, attended "Kid's Ecclesia," a 2night-3day spiritual formation retreat hosted by Promise Church, during the summer vacation and had a special encounter with the Holy Spirit. Considering that this was at age 9, I am reminded once again of the importance of the 4/14 Window-ages 4 to 14- which is highlighted in today's mission's strategy.

Since January 2018, Ellen has now been sown as "A seed of the Kingdom of God for Thailand". The remaining family of missionary Her will never be able to abandon the destiny of their calling in the land of Thailand. Life has given birth to life. Her sacrifice in the Lord will not be in vain (1 Cor.15:58). Amazing revival is sure to come in the predominantly Buddhist nation of Thailand. Especially, the next generation of Ellen's peers will experience a great revival and restoration. I ask you, readers of this book, to pray for this greater thing that are yet to come. Maranatha!

In the 2018 Christmas Season
Rev. Ben Yeonhaeng Hur,
Senior Pastor of Promise Church

God showed His mercy and love to Ellen Her through an extraordinary journey with Him to heaven and hell. The impact of her experience was intended not just for her but for many others, as I experienced in reading her story. The power of the testimony in this book will be a treasure for all who read it.

Burt Plaster,
Director of WEC-USA

"Heaven is about God's love"

The story of the Kingdom of Heaven in the confession of a child, though an easy read, this book has amazing Christian theological depth. Ellen shares hope of heaven in her own journey to a city of light and make heaven seem so real. We have felt deep sorrow for her parents in the loss of their beloved daughter, but we also have witnessed beauty blossoms from the greatest losses through their journey from grief to hope and trust in God in all circumstance.

We are the children of God and heaven is our home. And God said He has already prepared it for all of us.
What an amazing blessing!
I encourage you to join Ellen on her graceful journey.

Byungchil Bobby Kim,
Professor in Georgia Institute of Technology

Acknowledgements

I express my respect and honor to my fellow WEC International missionaries who have been working for many years in the mission fields of the world, leaving their familiar homeland and seeking lost souls with a pure passion to see God transform lives.

I would like to thank my beloved WEC USA missionaries, friends, and intercessors in Korea and USA for their valuable advice and encouragement.

I would also like to extend my heartfelt thanks to Elder Kwang Ho Lee and Marilyn Mertz, who have given so much of their time and effort in translating and editing and missionary Hey Jung Lee who has made the beautiful illustrations.

I would also like to show my appreciation to YKBooks,

Inc. in Korea for the producing and printing process of the books.

I would also like to thank Burt and Joni Plaster, who cared for us with counseling and prayer through our difficulties and hardships. Thanks also to my devoted wife, Ihnyoung, who always stands by me and our daughter Rin. You have endured courageously through our pain and loss.

I look forward to seeing you again soon, my beloved daughter Ellen, resting in heaven.
I give all the glory to the loving Lord Jesus who cares for us forever.

2018. November, Camp Hill , PA
Soosung Her

11

Table of Contents

Foreword /   6

Acknowledgements   10

Prologue   15

    Home-schooling   16

    Going to Thailand as Missionaries   20

Part 1. Entering Heaven   23

    1. Being Guided to Heaven's Gate   24

    2. Meeting God and Jesus   33

    3. Having My Sins Forgiven   38

    4. Meeting Adam   44

    5. Visiting My House   56

    6. Reading Books on the Bookshelf   65

    7. Having a Meal with Jesus   72

    8. Worshiping in Heaven   75

Part 2. Entering Hell 79

    1. The Burning Fire of Hell 80

    2. Disfigured Demons 84

    3. People Suffuring from Torture 87

    4. Hell, Where There is No Hope 90

Part 3. Coming Back 95

    1. Different Times 96

    2. It's Your Choice 100

    3. Crying a Lot 107

    4. Living for Jesus 111

Part 4. A Seed Planted for the Kingdom of God 115

    1. A Sudden Calling 116

    2. Hope for the Resurrection 124

    3. A Seed of the Kingdom of God 129

    4. What If... 141

    5. A Seed Begins to Bear the Fruit 146

    6. Leaving Herr Last Word 165

    7. Saying Goodbye 168

    8. Until We See You Again 184

Epilogue 187

Index of Scriptural References 194

About the Author 208

Ellen Her Foundation 210

M.K.
Planting Heaven

Prologue

Home-schooling

Going to Thailand as Missionaries

Prologue

Home-schooling

"Dad! God seems to be so pure because God only has light(1 John 1:5). There is only light in Him, and there is nothing of darkness in Him. But people are smaller than God, and their hearts are full of all kinds of bad and dirty things. God is light, and we are so dirty in His eyes. That is why we must pray to God and repent every time we sin, so that the light of God may come to us more and more."

A few days later, she said.

"Dad! There is really only light in heaven. Everywhere in heaven, everything is filled with light. There is no place for darkness because God is so full of light. Light keeps shining out from God. And the light from God is so bright, that the light makes all people clean."

When these mysterious and amazing words in the mouth of a child who was only eleven years old were pouring out like a waterfall, at first I thought,

"Did this child see a lot of strange movies?"

"Is there something wrong with her thinking?"

However, while continuing to listen to her story, I realized that the words she spoke were not made up but that she was sharing something she had experienced, vividly remembering it as if it happened yesterday. Many of the words she spoke were so realistic, giving so much detail, I knew that they could not have been made up by common sense or intellectual abilities of a child her age.

Typical of her peers, she was not an avid reader of the Bible. But after hearing her clear and vivid details of heaven and hell, I compared her account with the Bible and realized that she was not just making up stories to amuse her dad but was sharing her personal experience of visiting heaven and hell.

Ellen is now with the beloved Lord who hugged her so many times. Ellen is in heaven, home to which she wanted to return again. Ellen is a Missionary Kid. After a short thirteen- year journey that started in the United States, her body lies quietly in Tak, a small city in the middle of Thailand where her mother and I are ministering.

When she lived in New York with her father, mother and older sister, she never shared her testimony about this experience with her family. As a result, no one in our family knew about the fact that Ellen had gone to heaven and hell at the age of nine.

A few years ago, our whole family went to Thailand as a result of God's guidance, because we could not find a suitable school for Ellen in the Tak area, we had to homeschool her.

Before she began studying at home each morning, she read the Bible with dad and mom, and after meditations based on the reading for the day, she had time to share her insight. When we were sharing after reading the Bible, she told us that she was in heaven and hell during a church retreat in New York when she was a child. Now that Ellen has left, I write to share with you the memories of her vivid testimony.

Going to Thailand as Missionaries

Ellen was born in New York, eastern United States. She grew up spending most of her time in New York City where our family was involved in ministry. Our family member had immigrated to the U.S. from Korea years earlier, so Ellen enjoyed much time with her grandparents and uncle's family. She loved everyone and had a lot of fun making memories with family and friends.

God gave me a vision for missions early in my youth, but only when I was in the midst of my mid-forties did it come to fruition. At that time he called us to go to the mission field with a strong, clear vision. My wife and I decided to leave the United States, even though we had settled into a peaceful and comfortable life. By obeying the call, we went to Thailand, a huge Buddhist country that was totally unfamiliar to us and far from the U.S.A

To a nine-year-old girl, who had no idea what mission was at that time, God surprisingly revealed the reality of heaven and hell in a very specific and vivid way. I realize that the experience of seeing heaven and hell was God's loving and delicate love and compassion to prepare Ellen to live with the lost people of Thailand.

The Promise Church in New York City, where Ellen attended Sunday school, had an retreat annually for elementary school students. This retreat was held to help young students build up their faith through praise and prayer. It was called "Ecclesia" and Ellen went to this retreat at the age of nine.

A few days after the Ecclesia retreat began, a group of young children gathered at the chapel and prayed together. The boys began to pray together with the boys and the girls with the girls. Most of the lights in the small chapel were turned off and only a few lights were lit to light the surroundings. Music was turned on to help with prayer. Several teachers and youth pastors who participated in the program helped so that the children could concentrate fully on Jesus. With the background hymns, Ellen started to pray like the rest of the children.

Now let's hear Ellen's testimony.

Part 1.

Entering Heaven

1. Being Guided to Heaven's Gate

2. Meeting God and Jesus

3. Having My Sins Forgiven

4. Meeting Adam

5. Visiting My House

6. Reading Books on the Bookshelf

7. Having a Meal with Jesus

8. Worshiping in Heaven

Part 1. **Entering Heaven**

1. Being Guided to Heaven's Gate

As soon as I closed my eyes and prayed in the church chapel, suddenly someone grabbed my wrist. At the same time I was able to see vividly from above, myself in the purple t-shirt and pink pants that I like. I was praying. Suddenly my surroundings were filled with a white light that was brighter than the sun. The light was much brighter than the midsummer sunlight, which is so common on the earth. I could not open my eyes properly because it was too bright for my eyes. As I was going into heaven, suddenly a strong hand grabbed my wrist. I was surprised, but the moment, I felt that the Being who grabbed my wrist knew that I was afraid. I heard a vivid and clear voice.

"Do not be afraid."

I knew immediately that the person holding my hand was God without any explanation. I thought,

"Wow! This is amazing ...!"

For a moment, without time to think, in the blink of an eye, God took my hand and led me to the doors of heaven.

To my amazement, there were so many people in front of the gate of heaven that could not be counted. They were struggling to get into heaven. They were desperately trying to enter heaven, but even with their wholehearted effort, they could not go in. Some of the people who were gathered there were climbing up the heavenly door to try to get into, they were closed tightly before them. They were climbing up and falling over and over again. Others were banging on the door of heaven with their fists. They were screaming and shouting with despair and anger to have someone open the door. But in opposition to their efforts climbing up the walls of heaven and despairing cries, there was no response from inside the door of heaven.

Jesus said,

" … many will try to enter, and will not be able."

(Luke 13:24 NIV)

Heaven is not really a place that one can enter by his own efforts.

When I reached the door of heaven, I could see the door. The door was made of very large pieces of gold and jewels, and it was very high. The door looked so big and strong that it could not be opened or closed at will by people's power. But as soon as the God-holding my hands-reached the door of the Kingdom of Heaven, it opened like it knew who was standing there.

I was suddenly in heaven with God.

Even as I entered heaven, I was able to see many people knocking on the door with all their strength in desperation, begging and trying to open the door again and again. I asked God about those who are outside the door of heaven trying to get in.

"God, why can't they come into heaven?"

God responded very caringly,

"They have sinned. But they lied to me."

Suddenly an angel appeared to them as I was talking to God. Surprisingly, I could hear the angel talking to them.

The angel asked,

"Have you ever sinned?"

Many people answered the angel's question. Some said,

"No. I am so clean that I can enter heaven. I am very pure!"

It seemed everyone there was telling the angel that they were very pure.

The angel who heard their answers immediately told them,

"You are all lying!"

At that time, there was a book in the angel's hand, and the angel showed it to one of the many people who had been gathered there.

> "All the sins that you have committed are written here. Then you are lying when you say you have not sinned. You should have said, 'I have sinned. I am a sinner. Please forgive me for my sins.' Then we could have brought you to heaven. But since you lied, you cannot enter heaven."

The angel's answer was firm.

So many people were trying to enter the Kingdom of Heaven, but sadly, there was no one calling on the name of Jesus or asking Jesus for help. They just repeatedly tried to climb up the gate of heaven with their own strengths and efforts by knocking desperately on the heavily closed door. The angel who answered them moments before said,

> "You must believe in Jesus. Because Jesus died for you."

After hearing this, a man answered with his lips without believing in and trusting in Jesus.

"I believe it.
 I believe in it.
 I believe in whatever it is!"

He said this to the angel who was holding the book. He called Jesus, who is a person, "IT", which is used to refer to objects or things. When I heard his answer, I really felt sorry for Jesus. He called Jesus "IT ..."

He treated Jesus as an object that could be used and discarded depending on its usefulness. My heart hurt like it was tearing apart!

Those who were gathered outside the door of heaven were treating Jesus like a thing, using it according to their own needs, and then throwing it away whenever they didn't need it anymore.

Moreover, they thought of Jesus only as a tool or means to enter the Kingdom of Heaven, but not as a real person whom they could know and love.

The angel who heard it said,

"Do you consider Jesus as an IT? No!"

The angel was surprised to hear what this man said, treating Jesus as a thing.

"You cannot get into heaven."

He replied clearly, and then he left immediately.
After the angel disappeared, the people who had gathered there continued to do what they were doing. Some were still knocking on heaven's door, trying to enter heaven, yelling in a desperate voice, and others were trying to climb the door as before, but no one could enter it.

In New York, where I live, we get a lot of snow in winter. Sometimes, as if a hole in the sky had been punched out, we get so much snow that it reaches the knees of adults, and we have no school. We can't even leave the house. But after so much snowfall and many days of cleaning the snow, people start to go out to work and trample through the white snow. Cars that run on the road continue to crush the snow, and then the roads and the snow that is scattered on the streets become very dirty.

Suddenly, I saw a dark, grayish, dark cloud of color, similar to the dirty snow, near the people who were constantly struggling and screaming in front of the door of heaven. All of sudden the dirty, dark cloud instantly covered the people there, and a horrible-looking demon appeared and caught them all. The wretched demon that held onto those who were at the gate of heaven instantly fell with them back down to the place where the cloud first came.

When I went to hell with Jesus later, I saw a great many people there, and to my amazement, all those who were clamoring to open the door in front of the door of heaven were in hell.

I was led by the hand of God and passed through the gate of heaven, there was a man standing before me, dressed in a pure white dress with an incredibly bright light on his face and body. As soon as I saw Him, I recognized him as

Jesus-without a doubt. When I prayed in the chapel a little while ago, I was wearing purple clothes, but surprisingly, the clothes I was wearing now were changed as well.

I was in heaven and I was wearing a pure white dress that was brighter than snow, and the clothes were very beautiful. The white dress I was wearing in heaven was bright, beautiful and clean, unmatched by any clothes on the earth. No matter how beautifully you clean your clothes

in this world, you will not be able to get it that clean. The clothes were incredibly white and clean. Sometimes when my father preached, he said that all people who go to heaven would be wearing white clothes, and there I was, surprisingly dressed in a pure white dress mentioned in the scriptures! (Revelation 19:8).

2. Meeting God and Jesus

After entering into heaven led by God, I stood in front of Jesus. When I was at home and I was punished by my father or mother for doing something wrong, there was a time when I stood still with both hands by my side. When I stood for a long time, my feet and legs became very weak and painful. I stood in heaven for a while in front of Jesus, but I never felt my leg getting weak.

"Wow! My legs do not hurt at all!"

Amazingly in heaven, I could not feel any pain in my heart

or body at all.

Jesus, who was in front of me, was dressed in a pure white dress, and from his face, an incredibly bright light was flowing. Jesus, standing in front of me, was bright enough to make me blind. When I looked at Jesus' face, he looked so beautiful! Jesus had a nice beard. I saw the beautiful face of Jesus, and I saw a beautiful and magnificent crown that was placed on His head. The crown, something never seen on earth, was to indicate that Jesus was the Lord and king of this world and the Kingdom of Heaven. Actually, Jesus is the king of all of us.

When I said to Jesus,

"Thank you so much for inviting me to heaven."

Jesus Himself showed me his hands and feet. When I saw the hands of Jesus, I clearly saw nail marks in both of his hands. After that, my eyes naturally turned to Jesus' feet, and both feet had nail marks also. It was the side of Jesus that surprised me. There was a hole in his side. Later, I found out that the hole was the mark that was made when the Roman soldiers stuck the spear in Jesus' side while He was on the cross. The mark of the spear was clear on his side.

After I saw this, I remembered being told this story by my father. I realized that all of those wounds were traces of suffering that Jesus had endured on the cross for the sins of all of us, while He was here on earth. With the false accusation of the Jewish leaders, I realized that the Roman soldiers were the ones that put the nails in the very hands and feet of Jesus to hang Jesus on the cross. Indeed, Jesus had nail marks on his hands and feet as described in the Bible, and the nail marks were clear evidence of His crucifixion on behalf of us to pay the price for our sins. Jesus, who was crucified, died and was buried in the tomb of Joseph of Arimathea.

Surprisingly, Jesus who had been crucified for our sins did not stay buried in the grave, but rose again and now possesses a completely new body in heaven. Jesus, whom I met in heaven, was a person who had marks on His hands and feet and a sharp mark on His side. He overcame death and was resurrected, to have a whole new heavenly body and a crown. After I met Jesus with the nail marks and spear marks, I met God the Father.

God was sitting on a very large and high throne, and His majesty was magnificent. A beautiful and glorious light from His whole body was all around, and the light was filling the whole heaven. The light that flowed naturally from God was very beautiful. It was a light that people could not dare to imitate. How can I describe the light of heaven with any words of this world! The light was so bright and beautiful that as I was looking at God 's throne, I was overwhelmed and could not speak properly. I could not see the face of God because of the bright light, but He was sitting on the throne and really welcomed me.

In addition, Jesus was standing by the throne of God with great dignity. On the right side of the throne of God, there was also a throne of Jesus, whose throne was as great and magnificent as the throne of God. From the throne of the majestic Jesus, there continued to be light, and the light from it was so bright and pure that it seemed to me as if a wave of silver light was flowing. Through the light of God and Jesus' throne, the whole heaven was filled with light.

Because of that light, I could not see anything dirty or ugly in heaven, but only the clean, holy and bright things that filled the heaven. Because the light was shining all over the heaven, there was no darkness anywhere, and all the people and things in heaven were shining brightly.

3. Having My Sins Forgiven

Not long after I went to heaven, God placed his hand directly on my head. As soon as God put his hand on my head, all of my sins suddenly seemed to appear, and a transparent crystal ball appeared in front of me. With my eyes, I was able to clearly see blackish things inside the crystal ball. When I looked closely at them, I immediately knew that there were my sins. Although I was only a child of nine, I realized that they were all the sins I had committed while living on earth. These sins were all the sins I had committed knowingly and unknowingly. To my surprise, the sins seemed clear to my eyes. I could not pretend to deny the sins before God who showed them to me.

The fights and struggles with my older sister and the subsequent sins of hating her and cursing her in my heart were very clear. I also saw the sinful thoughts in my heart that I couldn't reveal to others because they were so hard to speak out. Being disobedient to my parents and being stubbornly resistant were other shameful sins.

When I saw the crystal ball filled with sins, my heart was heavy. In my heart I was already aware of my sins and prayed to Jesus for the forgiveness of my sins. When God knew that I was praying in my heart for the forgiveness of my sins, amazingly at that moment, God threw the crystal ball full of my sins into hell. When God threw the object like a crystal ball into hell, I saw an amazing sight. The mass of that sin was consumed by a demon in hell.

When God threw the ball, God completely forgave all my sins, as the Bible says. Just as the east and the west are far from each other, God threw all my sins far away. At that time, God spoke in an affirming voice,

"I forgive your sins."

As soon as I heard that God forgave all my sins, something amazing happened to me. When the object, like a crystal ball filled with sin, stood above my head, my heart was not peaceful and I felt heavy and uncomfortable. But after God forgave my sins and threw them away, I was very glad and my heart was as clear as a pure white feather dancing lightly in the sky. At the same time, like the calm of a still lake, the tremendous peace of heaven came down from God and filled my whole heart. I felt so happy and good! My heart, which was heavy, hard and uneasy until a little while before, was filled with incredible joy. The calmness, joy and happiness in the heavens filled my whole body and mind. Even now, I cannot express how happy and good I felt when I realized that God had forgiven my sins.

As soon as I heard the sweet and soft word that God forgave my sins, I immediately responded with excitement,

"Oh! God, thank you!"

God Himself knew all our sins. But instead of rebuking or reproving those who confess their sins in truth and turn from their sins in their heart, He comforts them and shows how good and compassionate He is. So after I had that amazing event where God himself forgave all my sins, I was able to travel with God to heaven. Heaven was not a small or narrow space as people often imagine. The heaven I experienced was very spacious. I couldn't see every area of heaven, but I couldn't help but notice that heaven was a much larger and bigger place than this world. After being forgiven of my sins, I saw the road of gold and walked the road together with God. The golden road was very big and beautiful! It was a road I have never seen in this world, but the golden road was all over heaven.

In heaven, there was an enormous number of angels, and the unusual thing was that several guardian angels guarded the people who came into the kingdom. In heaven, there were angels who had many other roles besides being guardian angels. I stayed in heaven and saw many angels, and every angel was working hard on their responsibilities. The angels I saw were really diverse in their work. Some angels seemed to be building homes. There were many houses already built in heaven, but still many angels were building more houses. I did not know where they got the materials to build a house, but the angels in charge of the building were working very hard. The houses they built were beautiful and magnificent. They built houses so lovely and cool that I felt it would be wonderful to live in such a house.

Then I saw other angel working, and they were carrying

loads of furniture carefully. Some of the angels were unloading items in the houses that were built. It seemed they were filling the houses with many things that were needed after the house was finished.

Some angels were around the throne of God. The angels stayed by the throne of God, praising the beauty of God and serving Him. There were angels who surrounded the throne of God, and other angels who play their instruments when all the people in heaven came to the throne of God to worship Him.

The angels I saw were not the kind that had a small, cute, powerless and weak appearance that looked like little babies we often imagined in childhood. Rather, all the angels looked bigger, stronger and cooler than the people who were in heaven. They were tall enough to help us at any time, and their bodies were very strong. What is surprising is that not a single angel in heaven was being lazy, but instead, diligently doing the things that were given to them.

Later I learned from my father the role of angels revealed

in the Bible. My father said that all the angels were sent by God to help people who believe in Jesus, not only in heaven but also on earth. The number of angels in heaven and on earth is great, and all of them are sent to help His people those who believe in Jesus. All the angels I saw in heaven were helping those who came up to heaven. Even though we cannot see them on earth, they are still here to

help adults and children. (Hebrews 1:14)

In this world, when we are faced with difficulties or danger, angels rescue believers from such hardships. Angels are always with us to protect us, but sometimes when we sin or do shameful things in the sight of God, they cover their faces with their wings. All the angels who are by our side to help us are holy and clean, so they do not want to see the wrong and dirty things that we do. They hide their faces or turn their faces away from our wrong actions. The reason we always have to be careful in this world is that the angels are aware over our actions, whether we sensed it or not.

4. Meeting Adam

When God forgave my sins and we walked the golden road together, I saw a man walking toward us. I was surprised that it was Adam, the first man to be created by the hand of God when He made this world.

The person I had studied about during Bible studies and heard preached about, was there standing in front of me.

I do not know how it happened, but as soon as I saw him, I immediately recognized him as Adam. Adam looked really cool and very young. It is recorded in Genesis that Adam lived over nine hundred years and died, so it is easy to think that Adam, would be old and wrinkled like a very old grandfather on earth, but surprisingly the Adam I met in heaven was a very strong and young man. I could not find in Adam any sign of old age, especially any sign of wrinkles.

What surprised me again was that Eve was next to Adam. Adam and Eve were walking on the golden path of heaven, talking to each other with affection. Both Adam and Eve who were walking the golden path of heaven were wearing pure white dresses, just like everyone else in heaven. I did not talk directly with Adam and Eve, but when I saw them, I could tell that they were Adam and Eve, the first people in the Bible.

Then I saw Moses with large animals that looked like lions and tigers. In this world, lions and tigers are animals that can sometimes be seen in the wilderness, but are so scary and wild that we should not get too close. I was very scared and afraid to see lions or tigers when I use to visit the zoo. Their roar was frightening. However, I met Moses with such animals and talked to him. Because I was always interested in animals, I approached Moses and asked him,

"What are you doing with these animals? Are you not scared?"

Moses replied,

"No animal in the Kingdom of Heaven will scare you away. These animals will not attack you. Lions, tigers or other animals will not frighten you. They are like dogs that are raised at home in the world. Do you want to touch them?"

I stroked an animal similar to a tiger, and the animal's hair was very soft and nice. Besides, the animal did not threaten me at all, and he was a very nice and good animal.

I like puppies, cats and other animals very much. Unfortunately, even though I like animals so much, I could not have puppies at home. I used to go around the neighborhood and pet dogs or cats without my parents knowing. However, when I touched a cat or a puppy on earth, my face would quickly get red and develop hives. I would cough constantly because I have an allergy to animal fur. If I touch or pet the animals, especially puppies, quickly my face gets red with an allergic reaction and my whole body becomes itchy. That is the reason why my dad and mom did not like me touching animals and would frequently remind me not to touch them. If I touched a puppy, no matter how I tried to hide it, my face and body would react, so my mom would immediately tell me to take a bath and give me allergy medicine.

To my astonishment, my allergies completely disappeared in heaven. I could touch an animal similar to the tiger that Moses had. I stroked the animals and I liked them very much. They did not threaten or bother me and my face and body did not react, so I was pleased.

In heaven, everyone was happy and healthy without any illness or pain. Unlike hell, in heaven, I could not see anyone physically or mentally sick. Everyone was living a healthy and physically able life.

Dad later explained about the people who live in heaven. When we go to heaven, our bodies are completely different from on the earth, and our bodies will be without illness or pain. We will have a very healthy and sturdy body. He also explained that in heaven we will be changed into the most healthy and beautiful existence. Even children who go to heaven when they are small are made whole. People living there are healthy, without disease or pain. Those who come to heaven at a later age-those who have had disabilities from birth, or from the accident-when they come to heaven, their bodies will turn into a whole new heavenly body. They will live in a most beautiful way. My dad told me that there will be no embarrassment or bad feelings about physical damages or faults. He explained that we would live in heaven with the most beautiful and wonderful appearance. All the people I met in Heaven, starting with Adam, turned out to be beautiful and healthy. In addition, our consciousness will be a thousand times clearer than now so we will recognize people as soon as we see them. Whenever I met someone in heaven, I could immediately recognize who they were without Jesus or an angel explaining them to me. And when I actually saw Adam, Eve and Moses, I could recognize right away who they were. After seeing Adam and Moses, I met other people.

When I entered heaven, I could not see my dad, my mother or my older sister Rin because our family did not die, but was still living in this world. After meeting and talking with Adam, Eve and Moses, God said to me,

"I will surprise you."

I was very curious after hearing this. At that moment, I was standing in front of my grandmother's father-my great-grandfather-who had died in New York City, when I was very young. As soon as I saw my great-grandfather, I said,

"Grandpa! I missed you!"

And as soon as my great-grandfather saw me, he said,

"Oh, Ellen!"

Then my great-grandfather came and hugged me. When he died in this world, my great-grandfather was the father of my grandmother. He was almost 90 years old. His back was always bent, and he had no strength in his body. He always walked slowly and carefully, and he could not digest food properly, so he was really weak and powerless. He only ate a little each day. Sometimes when I visited him, because he had no strength, he just sat down on the chair and asked me to bring him things. He also had a lot of wrinkles on his face, and he could not see well with his eyes, so he always wore thick black glasses.

In heaven my great-grandfather was very young. He had no wrinkles on his face; he was very dignified and gorgeous like a strong and sturdy young man, and he did not wear those thick glasses that he used to wear all the time on earth.

There was a beautiful woman standing by my great-grandfather. He said to me,

"This is your great-grandmother."

I had never seen my great-grandmother on earth because my great-grandmother was already dead before my mother was born. My great-grandmother died of sickness when my grandmother was nine years old. My great-grandmother, who my mother never saw, was standing beside my great-grandfather. My great-grandmother in heaven was a beautiful and pretty lady. She looked a lot like my grandmother in New York, and she had short, curly hair. She was wearing a white dress and was really young and beautiful. My great-grandmother was beside my great-grandfather and she gave me a bright smile.

After a pleasant meeting with my great-grandfather, I was walking along the road to heaven, and the Lord pointed to another person and said to me,

"He is the first missionary to Thailand."

"God,"

I said,

"I do not even know him. Why are you introducing me the first missionary who went to Thailand?"

God answered,

"You will know very soon the reason why you are meeting him."

At that time, my dad and mom were busy with ministry in New York. They did not think about missions at all because they were totally engaged in serving the church in New York City. Therefore, they could not really be concerned about Thailand, so I did not know anything about Thailand at that time. Presently, they are ministering as missionaries in Thailand, but back then it was a nation not in their thoughts.

Now that I think about it, though I did not know at the time why God had me meet a missionary who first came to Thailand to preach the gospel, it was His plan to show me the person who went to Thailand before us. The greatness and mercy of God, who knows all the past, present and future of a person, is truly amazing.

Sometimes, we do not understand at the time when we encounter some unexpected people or circumstance, but as time goes on, we understand better. There is no mistake or coincidence in God's plans. God always has an exact plan for each person, and according to that plan, He allows us to meet other people or prepares a special environment for us.

Oh! What a wonderful surprise. We do not know what is happening up ahead, but God knows everything. He even knew everything that will happen in our future.

In heaven, as soon as we see a person, we can recognize each other without explanations. There was no sadness or anxiety for those who lived in heaven, and I was in such a state that I was filled with happiness and joy. So it was a great pleasure to meet people in heaven.

During the trip to heaven, I cried because heaven was so good, and I was so happy to be there.

And above it all, I felt,

"Here is my real dad."

and I realized,

"God is my true father."

When I was so happy that I was shedding tears of joy, God hugged me and said.

"I know you well. When people come to heaven, many of them shed tears of joy like you. I am already familiar with it. It's okay. You can cry out loud."

He encouraged me. Usually when I cried on earth, my mom and dad and others would feel uncomfortable and annoyed and say,

"Stop crying! Stop crying!"

But in heaven, God said,

"It's okay!"

It was a big comfort to me.

Tears continued to flow in my eyes, but the tears were not so much tears of sorrow, but tears of joy and happiness.

I was happy because He was the true Father God who made me and knows me best and cares for me. Even now, when I think about God and Jesus in heaven, I want to see God and Jesus again. Without realizing it, I sometimes shed a tear.

5. Visiting My House

In the Bible, Jesus told his disciples that he would ascend to heaven after His death on the cross and be resurrected on the third day. The disciples of Jesus who heard His words worried about not being able to see Him anymore. To those concerned and anxious disciples, Jesus comforted them and said,

"My father's house are many rooms; if it were not so, I would have told you. I am going there to prepare a place for you. And if I go and prepare a place for you, I will come back and take you to be with me that you also may be   where I am."

(John 14: 2,3 NIV)

After He had given this promise to His disciples, He was crucified and died, as He had said, and resurrected on the third day. He showed Himself to His disciples for forty days and ascended into heaven. Jesus in heaven is preparing a place for all Christians to dwell in.

After meeting many people in heaven, Jesus led me to another place. Jesus, who led me there, said,

"This is the house where you will live when you come back to heaven in the future."

It was a really nice and spacious house. The house was all built of gold. It was a single floor, and as I walked into the house, everything was neatly arranged, and the furnishings I would needed were well prepared everywhere. There was a neatly arranged bed. The bed was made of gold and looked very soft and comfortable. Sometimes on earth, I used to be frightened when I had to sleep by myself and had to go to the restroom in the middle of the night.

So I asked Jesus,

"Is there any fear in heaven? When I sleep alone in my room, I feel awful and sometimes I have bad dreams."

Jesus answered,

"In heaven, there is no more fear or bad dreams."

After hearing Jesus' words, I lay down on the bed in my room for a moment. One of the guardian angels that was caring me lay down beside me. When the angel lay beside me there was no fear of anything at all, and it felt very familiar.

The angel who lay beside me said,

"No one has bad dreams in heaven."

I was in my heavenly home for a while, and as I lay down on my bed, I did not feel any dread or fear at all. On the contrary, my heart was calm and peaceful. Since God was with me in the Kingdom of Heaven, no fear came into my heart, but the amazing peace that God gave me was warmly enveloping my whole heart and body. I could feel the peace and quietness that Jesus gave me with His presence. So I lay down in bed and looked around the room where I would be staying in the future.

What was unusual was that when I looked around the

house, I couldn't see a kitchen. In this world I have to make food to eat every day, so I need a kitchen, but I do not need to make the food in heaven, so it was okay not to have a kitchen.

There was a bookcase near the living room in the house. The bookcase was very big and was not empty, but filled with lots of books. Also, there was a door to the back of the house and when I opened the door, I saw a very large garden out in the back. There I could grow a beautiful garden and raise as many animals as I wanted. There were other houses beside the house where I stayed. When I met the people next door, I did not have to ask for their name but I knew who they were. I saw someone was raising animals in their backyard, and another was growing all kinds of beautiful flowers. It was so colorful and beautiful to see the flowers they were growing! All of the flowers were in full bloom and they filled the whole garden. My heart was filled with happiness in seeing the garden. The guardian angels that were there to help me were standing at the entrance to my house-two at the entrance, and two others at the back door. While I was in heaven, they were always there to take care of me.

I saw an enormous number of angels in heaven. There were so many angels that they could not be counted. They were helping and guiding those who came to heaven. There were four guardian angels beside each person. They were guiding people and went with them wherever they went. When I saw the houses of people in heaven, there were two guardian angels in front and back respectively.

Each angel had wings and were taller, bigger and stronger than people. They were not like the men or women we see in the world where we live now. I could not distinguish angels by gender but all the angels seemed attractive.

Behind the houses where people lived, was a very large garden-like space. I want to raise animals very much. Especially when I pet animals, I feel great. When I was with Jesus in my house garden, I asked,

"Jesus. I want to raise a lion here. Can I raise a lion?"

Jesus tenderly said,

"Of course you can."

As soon as I heard that, I was excited. While living on earth I really liked puppies and wanted to raise puppies, but because my body was allergic to animal hair, and because of asthma, I could not grow puppies. I really wanted to raise a puppy, so I often nagged my mom and dad, but I was refused many times.

When I went to Tak province in Thailand, I raised rabbits a few times instead of dogs while I was home - schooling alone. I was so excited and happy when my dad bought me my first rabbit at the Saturday market in Tak.

When my family lived in New York, I could not raise a puppy because of allergies, so my sister and I put two turtles in a small aquarium and raised them. At first, my grandmother bought two turtles that were smaller than a bird 's finger, so I nurtured them with all my heart. After I raised them for a few years, the two tortoises were as big as the palm of my hand. It was a great joy and pleasure for my sister and I to take care of the turtles living in the aquarium.

When I had to leave for Thailand with my parents, I

could not bring the two turtles, so I had to give them to my mom's friend. Because I had such fond memories of raising turtles, I wanted to raise an animal in Thailand.

Because my sister was away studying in Chiang Mai and I was home-schooling without any friends, I was very bored and wanted to raise animals. I was very happy to buy a rabbit, but soon the rabbit was weak and suddenly died. I was so sad and I cried a lot. Because I was so sad to see the dead rabbit, I asked my dad to make a grave for my rabbit in the side yard. I made a cross with a small tree on top of the grave. After that, I made another trial raising rabbits.

I bought another baby rabbit at Saturday market and tried to raise him, but the rabbit died.

I tried one more time but unfortunately that rabbit died too, so I had to give up raising rabbits.

When I was in heaven, Jesus allowed me to have a lion as a pet. The lion was not a scary or fearful creature like on earth, but a cute and loving creature that poses no danger or harm. When I was allowed to have a lion in my house in heaven, my heart was really joyful and thankful.

After I looked around the house prepared for me in heaven, my heart was very happy. When I saw the house, I realized how well Jesus knew my taste. The house was furnished to my liking and it was well prepared for all my needed. Also, my house in heaven was big enough to be compared to any house in the world. The house was very big and I could see that it had plenty of rooms. I was happy thinking about living there in the future. I liked the house so much I just wanted to stay there.

After looking around my house, I saw houses next to mine that were prepared for my sister, mom and dad. What was surprising was that my father, mother and sister, Rin, were not yet in heaven but were still living on earth. In heaven their houses were already prepared for them. Although I did not go and look around the houses, the houses were big and wonderful like my house. I was very happy thinking about living in heaven with my sister, mom and dad.

6. Reading Books on the Bookshelf

As I walked into my house that Jesus showed me, there was a bookcase next to the living room wall. The bookshelf was also made of gold. What I saw was a six-shelf bookcase, in which each shelf was packed, and the books were neatly organized.

I picked up one of the books in the first section and read it. It was a record of my life. Amazingly, while I lived on earth, it was written in detail about many of the actions I have done in this world. I did not read all the books on the first shelf, but as soon as I saw them, I recognized that they were all about my life. They had detailed records of my actions and thoughts while living on earth. However, while reading the book, I was not embarrassed or ashamed about the content of the book.

There were several books in the next section, which contained books regarding my mom, dad, and my sister Rin. The record of our family life while we lived on earth was carefully written. While living in New York with my mom, dad and my sister, we made lots of happy memories.

In the third section there were books written about the relatives around me. The book detailed the people I know on the earth who can be called relatives and who have direct or indirect affiliations with me. There are details about grandparents and relatives in Korea as well as grandmother and grandfather in the United States.

The fourth and fifth sections were books related to people I lived with and met living on earth-my friends, teachers, church friends and youth pastors I met while I was in church. There were a full record of church members and people who were associated with me in any place throughout my life.

The special thing was the last shelf. There were books on that sixth shelf. But when I saw the books of that shelf, the contents of the books were all empty. In addition, there was a table or desk- like object made of gold next to the bookcase. When I looked at the desk, there were many blank papers left on the desk, with a stack of paper like a book.

"Jesus, why are these books empty?"

I asked.

Unlike other books, nothing was written in them. I wondered about those empty books and that is why I asked Jesus.

"You can write in heaven. It's like writing a diary. After you write it, you can put it on the last shelf."

Jesus responded affectionately.

When I talked to my dad about this experience during one of our home-schooling sessions with my mom and dad at Tak, my dad explained to me that it was easy to understand the contents of books I saw on the heavenly bookshelf. There are books in heaven about each person, and that book is called the book of deeds. The book of deeds is a detailed account of a person's thoughts and deeds while living on earth. The book records all the good and bad acts that each person has done, and all thoughts in the subconscious are recorded as well. The book also records the careless jokes that people make without thinking. Surprisingly, the book records all the thoughts of their minds in full detail (Matthew 12:36).

After looking through the many books on my bookshelf in my house in heaven, Jesus told me about some of the painful things I experienced during my school days in the United States. My experience at America school was so hard and heartbreaking to me many times and Jesus explained to me about it.

When I was in elementary school in the United States, I had a friend in my class. Her name was S, and she hurt me very badly. Sometimes she lied to my teacher and got me in trouble, other times she made life difficult for me and hurt my feelings. Whenever I thought about S, my heart was troubled, and even I didn't want to go to school. Many times, I thought about ways to get revenge on S. But, in my house in heaven, Jesus Himself spoke to me.

"I know your pain. I know who is troubling you. I will give you comfort."

Jesus surprised me with His intimate knowledge of my difficulties and suffering from others. He even knew exactly who was troubling me, how they gave me pain, and even the names of the person who was hurting me. When Jesus said that, my heart was much relieved. My former thought of getting revenge on S also disappeared in an instant. As soon as Jesus comforted me, I was happy and at the same time my heart was full of joy. In my heart was born a feeling of forgiveness and compassion for S who hurt me.

Living in this world sometimes we meet people who hurt us and make life hard for us. Every time we meet such people we have to have pity them and forgive their mistakes, but it's never easy to truly forgive those who are troubling and distressing us. It is impossible by our will and effort. But if we bring our pain and hardship to Jesus, Jesus himself will comfort us. Then God gives us a heart that can pity on them and forgive them rather than seeking revenge. True forgiveness in this world does not come from ourselves. It is only possible when we have the heart of God. Then we can not only forgive people but live in this world with the joy and peace in our hearts that comes from heaven.

After that, God took me to where His throne was, and there was another book.

"I know all the names of the people in this book, and they know who I am."

God said.

I saw that this was *The Book of Life* that had the names of those who believed in Jesus and were saved.

Jesus, the Good Shepherd said,

"I know the names of the sheep and my sheep know me."   (John 10:14)

He said very clearly that the people in *The Book of Life* -those whose names are written there, also know who God is.

The surprise is that no one could write his name in the book that God Himself held; only God could record it. It was astonishing that when God recorded in *The Book of*

Life, it was not with a pen or pencil like on earth. Just thinking it in His mind was enough for it to be written.

7. Having a Meal with Jesus

After traveling for a while in heaven, Jesus said,

"Let's go to have a meal together."

There was a very big table in the place that Jesus led me to. I saw the table, and the food was beautifully set. As if a big party was being held at the big banquet hall. The table was filled with delicious and scrumptious food. It was a most magnificent banquet. There was a very high and nice chair at the table that reminded me of a movie scene. The chair was very beautiful and quite high in appearance. When I sat on the chair to eat the variety of foods on the table, I felt like a princess, and I was actually treated as such. Jesus treated me like a princess at the table. I suddenly felt that

"God is really my true father"

and

"I do not want to leave my good father."

The food on the table was plentiful and nicely done like a big banquet feast. It was such a great and wonderful meal as if we had gathered all the delicious food from around the world. Among the foods that were prepared, I saw some noodle foods looks like spaghetti from the United States and foods similar to noodles in Korea. So I wanted to eat that food like spaghetti. When I ate the food, it was so delicious that I could not really explain it.

My mother often served delicious food at home for our family, and the food she served was wonderful, but the food I ate in heaven was really delicious and wonderful that it could not compare with any food I had eaten on earth. It was so delicious that I quickly finished my first bowl. After eating a bowl, I asked,

"Jesus! Can I have another bowl?"

Jesus answered,

"Sure, you can eat as much as you can."

I emptied the second bowl, and then another three bowls in all. It was really delicious, and I could feel the joy of my fullness. I was very happy that I was invited to a meal with Jesus in heaven and that I could eat the food of heaven.

There was even honey in heaven. It looked so delicious, I tried it once. The taste was very sweet that it could not be compared to any honey on earth. As I tasted it, I wanted to just keep eating more and more. I was so happy and joyous after eating with Jesus for such a long time.

In the Psalms or Revelation, God invites Christians to the table of God, eating and drinking with them. After eating with Jesus in heaven, when I came back to the earth, I found out that what was recorded in the Bible was not just a parable, but that we will actually eat and drink at the table with Jesus in heaven (Rev. 3: 20). I also found that being invited to the table was not only a glorious privilege but also a joyful and happy occasion.

8. Worshiping in Heaven

This time I was led to the throne of God in heaven. Numerous angels surrounded the majestic throne of God, and among them was an angel who was in charge of music and another angel was tuning a harp. The sound of the harp was very beautiful.

God had His own timetable for world events. God's timetable was like a calendar made of gold. I did not know what was written in the timetable, but I thought it would probably record the events that would happen in heaven and on earth. When we gathered together and worshiped together, it was not Sunday or the Lord's Day like the day we worship on earth. Exactly speaking, there was no Sunday or Lord's Day in heaven. Every day was a special day, and at any time we could worship God with joy.

God asked me,

"Will you come to worship with me?"

I replied,

"Yes, God, of course. Of course!"

God sat on His throne at the time of worship and was pleased with the prayers and praises of the many people around Him. I was so excited that I sang many hymns with the people gathered there. In the place where we worshiped, I could see not only people worshiping but also many angels worshiping God. It was holy and magnificent. What was surprising was that although each person was worshiping in a different language, the communication between them was natural, and God knew all the languages. Even the people who gathered there spoke to each other in their different languages, but they did not have any difficulty in understanding each other's minds. On earth, it is frustrating at times when we do not understand each other because of our different languages, but in heaven God knows all the languages. In heaven we are sons and daughters of God and have God's DNA, so we worship and communicate in English, Spanish, Japanese, Korean and many other languages. And there is no difficulty in understanding each other. Rather, as soon as we have a conversation, we can easily understand each other.

In the book of Revelation, it says that in the Kingdom of Heaven, all of the tribes, tongues and nations in the kingdom will come to God and worship him (Revelation 7:9). There I was and it was actually happening around me. I was very happy and joyful when I saw the scene of the beautiful worship where all the people worshiped the living God with one heart and in one accord-each in their own language.

In this world, I sometimes disliked and felt it was a bother to read the Bible, pray and go to worship. But in heaven, with all the angels and the people gathered there, it was the most joyous and fascinating time. It was wonderful and beautiful worship that was very different from the worship services on earth. I do not know how long I was in heaven, but while I was in heaven I was never thirsty. I did not feel thirsty at all because heaven was filled with every good thing and being with God was in itself happiness, joy and fulfillment.

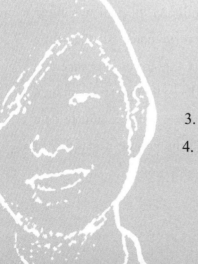

Part 2.
Entering Hell

1. The Burning Fire of Hell

2. Disfigured Demons

3. People Suffuring from Torture

4. Hell, Where There is No Hope

Part 2. **Entering Hell**

1. The Burning Fires of Hell

After having a wonderful time in heaven with Jesus, He suddenly took me to hell. As I went into hell, I realized that my feet did not touch the ground. It felt as though my feet and those of were floating on the clouds. Amazingly, I could see hell vividly in front of my eyes.

Hell was very wide. Heaven was, of course, much bigger than hell, and as I already mentioned, heaven was filled with many beautiful things everywhere. At the same time, each person in heaven was able to live in peace and happiness in a well-built house. Even though hell was such a big place, all the space was open without any private resting place and no houses. All the people who suffered there could look at each other's afflictions.

Hell was wrapped in darkness everywhere. When I went to heaven, the light that flowed from God filled the heavens and the whole place was really bright and shining. The darkness had no place because the bright lights illuminated everything everywhere in heaven. In contrast to heaven, hell was dark everywhere, and I could not see any light similar to what I saw in heaven. The deep darkness covered all of hell, so I was really depressed and felt creepy just being there.

Jesus once shared a parable of the kingdom. It was about a king giving a marriage feast. He told the servants to go out and invite the people, but the invited guests refused the king's invitation with many excuses. At that point the king commanded his servants to go to the mountains and fields and bring other people to the feast. Among the many people that attended the feast, there was a man who came in without an appropriate clothing. When the king saw that man, he commanded his servants to throw him outside into the darkness which represents hell as written in the Word of God (Matthew22:13). There is no doubt that the hell is a place filled with a deep darkness-a place with no hope.

In the Bible, Jesus said that people who do not believe in him are the children of darkness. In their minds, such people think all kinds of dark thoughts and justify actions of darkness. Because they are children of darkness, there is no true light in their lives. They are influenced by hell's darkness, whether they know it or not.

Because the devil and his demons that are his henchmen live in the darkness of hell, everything they think and act is from the darkness. On this earth, people who controlled by demons join them in wicked acts. The devils and demons in hell have no light whatsoever. The darkness in the hell is real and it was not simply a symbol or an imagination, but a place filled with darkness with no light. I was really scary and terrifying.

Another surprise was that there was no water or food to eat in hell. Many in hell were begging and asking for water because of thirst, but I could not see a single drop of water in hell and there was no trace of water.

When I was invited to the table in heaven that Jesus led me to, there was a great variety of delicious food at the table.

But there was no food in hell. It was completely opposite to heaven where I could eat or drink as much as I wanted. All the people in hell were suffering from hunger.

In heaven there was a very soft, warm bed made of gold in my house, but in hell there was no bed. That's why people were suffering and could not rest at all. It was a terrible and horrible place where I could never expect to rest or relax.

A lot of people filled in the wide space of hell. There was an enormous number of pillars to bind people in the large open space. When I saw those people in hell, I saw that all of them to poles made of something like thick iron or steel so they could not move. And all around them was burning fire. As if to swallow everything, the hot flaming fire never ceased to turn off, and all the people in hell screamed in constant pain and thirst because of the hot fire that continued to burn. (Mark 9:43b)

In spite of such agonizing screaming, no one offered a bowl of water in hell. No sip of water was allowed there, but only fire, fire, fire, which would never ceased. Nothing but the blazing fire was burning all the time in hell, and the people were suffering in the midst of it. That was the hell I saw.

Just being in hell was scary and frightening. When I was so afraid of seeing such a sight, Jesus hugged me because He understood all my fears. Then the feeling of fear and sacredness disappeared, and with the relief of Jesus being by my side, my mind became calm again.

2. Disfigured Demons

I could see many demons in hell. The demons in hell were all strange and disfigured. Not one of the demons I saw was attractive or proportional. The appearance of the demons in hell was exactly the opposite of the beautiful and handsome appearance of the angels in heaven. They are as unbalanced and unusual as the pictures that a little boy who does not know how to draw, draw in an unusual way. I could see the faces of the demons in hell, and their faces were very ugly. When one eye was crooked, the other half looked like it was almost floating out of the socket. The ears were torn on one side, the other was missing, and the mouth was strangely twisted. Even the nostrils were not balanced. I looked at the body of the demons, but the arm was either missing or strangely distorted, so it looked really ugly. There were many demons, but not a single one proportionally balanced.

I did not feel good looking at those ugly demons, but what I hated was that the demons had a very disgusting and dirty smell coming out from them. The smell from them was so nasty that I did not want to breathe. These dirty and disgusting smells did not come out only once but continued to flow out of them. Furthermore, these odors from the demons were filling the whole of hell, and many people were groaning in pain in hell. It was so dark, dirty and very disgusting.

In the Bible, there are frequent occasions when Jesus heals people with disabilities. Among them were the blind, the paralyzed, and those who could not walk. He also delivered people from demons who were tormenting them.

But when Jesus cast out demons, He often referred to them as "unclean spirits" (Mark 1:26), and the demons I saw in hell were actually dirty and ugly. They were so disgusting and smelly that I was shocked just by looking at them.

When we see people on earth who do not believe in Jesus and live in their own way, they are living under the influence of unclean spirits, though they are not aware of it themselves. In fact, I think that the dirty lives of those who do not know Jesus, creating lies, making bad movies, murdering and betraying are based on the influence of those wicked spirits that smell.

If heaven is the place where the blood of Jesus forgives sins, and where only clean people go, hell is a place where they live with their filthy sins. The things I saw in hell were so dirty and disgusting that I really do not want to even remember it.

3. Suffering Torture

After seeing the demons, I saw people in hell. The people who were trying to climb the heavenly gate and knocking on the door of heaven when I first went to heaven's gate were all in hell. The people in hell were all tied to the iron-like poles. I was able to see the people who were there in detail. They were all naked and their bodies were really bony because they did not eat anything at all. They were all tied up without hope and in terrible pain. There was burning fire all around them, and there were a lot of spooky demons surrounding them. But the demons surrounding them were brutally torturing those who were tied to poles. The demons were punishing them for the sins and crimes they had committed while on earth.

I was able to get a closer look at how a person was being tortured. I did not know exactly what sins the person had committed on earth, but it seemed it had something to do with lying. The many demons surrounding him were constantly cursing and tormenting him with the very same lies that the man had told on earth. It wasn't hard to see that just hearing the curse of the demons was enough causing him a great deal of mental suffering.

Like in heaven, our senses in hell are a thousand times more sensitive than on earth. So when this man heard such curses, he felt so much pain that he shouted out in torment. As soon as one demon had finished torturing him, another demon came out, and this time he started poking him with a spear. I did not know exactly what he had done wrong on earth, but the other demon continued to stab and torture him. Every time he was stabbed, he screamed with tremendous pain, but no one had mercy on him. Even Jesus, who brought me to hell, was only silent there. When the torture of each demon was over, the next demon would come, and then the next. He was not given any rest and was constantly tortured. It was obvious that the man was suffering from so much torture.

I saw another man tied to a strong pole like a metal. He seemed to be a bully who harassed people he thought were weaker than he was while he was on earth. Surprisingly, in hell he was being beaten by the demons.

Those who were tied there were repaid in hell according to what they had done on earth. The people who were tied up on the poles were suffering so much! They were groaning in hell with tremendous torture from the demons, and I saw no one who was healthy or well. Everyone in hell looked like a person with a disability, and their appearance looked very ugly like the demons. Some people were blinded by the torture of the demons, and their ears and mouth were also severely torn and hurt. I felt that the sufferings of those who suffered in hell were so severe that I wished it could be over. But it was very sad and frightening that there was no death in hell. People were to suffer forever. I was so frightened and scared that I really did not want to remember them again, so I held onto Jesus who was next to me.

Sometimes I remembered this scene even after returning from heaven. Every now and then, when I think about the endless torture and the pain they have to endure, I get chills.

4. Hell, Where There is No Hope

Whether someone sinned knowing or unknowingly, in hell they had to pay the price for their actions. In the hot fire that Jesus described was for all eternity. People were groaning in pain in hell, and they had no hope in that darkness.

Hell is!

A place full of darkness.

A place where hot fires keep burning.

A place where you continue to suffer from constant thirst.

A place where not even a sip of water is allowed.

A place where pain and fear never cease.

A place you can never break out.

A place

Where the dirty and disgusting smell of demons constantly flows,

Whether you like it or not, the smell persists.

Where people are constantly suffering and being tortured for their sins.

Where there is no mercy and compassion.

Where you have to stay forever.

Where people suffer not for 100 years, 1000 years, 10000 years, but all eternity.

A cursed place where you have to stay endlessly.

Where there is no hope or possibility of escape.

This is hell.

Heaven is truly a place filled with light, happiness and joy by the light of God, but hell has no hope or deliverance from the deep darkness. It was only a place of tremendous pain, cruelty and terrible curses. No matter what, no one should ever come to a terrible place!

When I visited hell with Jesus, we floated above the ground. Fortunately, we did not set our feet in hell. Jesus explained the reason saying,

"Anyone who puts their feet on the ground in hell

belongs to hell."

If there are people you know who think lightly about hell, we who believe in Jesus should really tell them the reality and fear of the hell.

The hell I witnessed was not just an idea that pastors and Christians thought up or invented to scare people to believe in Jesus. In fact, hell is real, and the appearance of hell was so terrible, scary and frightening that the people who fell into it came to realize that no matter how well they had lived, how rich or how smart they were, they are under the cursed.

After visiting hell, I began to consider what being blessed and being cursed is about. It is really unfortunate that those who are beautiful, smart and famous but do not know Jesus remain under the curse. Because they are not forgiven for their sins, they will be forced to spend eternity in punishment in hell. On the other hand, those who know Jesus and live for Him as their Lord are set free from the curse and will go to heaven and be with Him, forever enjoying His blessings.

Heaven and Hell.

There is such an obvious difference; one was a place I have to go no matter what the cost and the other was a place I would avoid at all cost.

I understood deep within that heaven is not just a matter of our choosing, but I am willing to sacrifice whatever it takes to be able to take my place there.

M.K.
Planting Heaven

Part 3.

Coming Back

1. Differnt Times

2. It's Your Choice

3. Crying a Lot

4. Living for Jesus

Part 3. **Coming Back**

1. Different Times

I do not know how long I stayed in heaven, but when I came back to the retreat center, it felt like a long time. It was not hard to realize that a few hours on earth was actually a fairly long time in heaven. There are hours, minutes and seconds on the earth, but in fact there is no concept of time in heaven, so it may not be possible to compare the time on earth with time in heaven. Many of the experiences I had during my stay in heaven were so happy for me that the times in heaven felt short.

When we watch an interesting and funny movie or play a fun game, we feel like time passes by without us realizing it. On the other hand, if you do not have much interest, and have to be part of things you do not enjoy, or if you see a movie that is not funny, you can easily feel bored and think,

"Why does time go so slowly?"

Some of the times in our daily life in this world are enough to raise our expectations and excitement, and these are moments of joy and happiness. However, most of the things we experience or do in our daily lives are in fact too boring to enjoy. So some people often say,

"I do not like life in the world."

But life in heaven was so different from life in the world that every moment was a series of joyful and interesting things. While I was in heaven, I completely forgot about time, and I did not even think of looking for a clock and did not think about time itself.

Some people may think,

"If I go to heaven, I will worship every day, so how fun would that be?"

In fact, life in heaven was not boring or without fun as some people imagine. Of course we have time to worship God, but even times of worship were fun and exciting. During worship in heaven, angels and all who are in heaven worship together, unlike worship on earth. It is lively and dynamic worship. Because our worship is in front of God and Jesus, who receive our worship, from their majestic throne, every moment of worship is full of joy and happiness. The time we worship in heaven is the time when everyone in heaven is renewed moment by moment and filled with the light given by God. It is not boring or dull! The more I worshiped, the more joy and happiness I felt. That is why worship in heaven is a truly exciting and amazing experience for everyone to rejoice together.

In heaven we can do many other things besides worshiping. I was able to do a variety of things in my own home, such as gardening, raising my animals, playing music, and writing. In addition, we can spend time with people we want to spend time and get to know more people. Heaven really made me excited and interested in returning.

That is why when He said that I needed to go back, I begged God to let me stay. I really can't wait to go back to heaven because there are so many fun and exciting things to do in heaven.

Paul, a disciple of Jesus-after he experienced heaven-said that he would like to go to heaven quickly if he could. He said that he desired to be with the Lord. Later he was martyred for the sake of the gospel of Jesus and entered heaven. I understand his desire to be with the Lord.

Heaven really is such a joyful place that no one would want to leave once they experience it. No one who enters heaven wants to leave, but rather they want to live there forever. In heaven we transformed into a whole new person and new body, and live a life that is completely different from the life we live in this world.

On the other hand, life in hell was so painful-so full of pain and punishment that I don't even want to think about it. I didn't want to stay there for one second. The fact that one has to stay forever in such a terrible and scary place is truly sad.

As it is written in the Bible,

> "A day is like a thousand years and a thousand years
> are like a day" (2 Peter3:8).

I think we live for a long time when we live in this land for about 100 years, but actually it is a short moment of time compared to the time in heaven. This world passes by quickly, but heaven is a place to live forever.

2. It's Your Choice

After visiting hell, Jesus and I returned to heaven. Because hell was so scary and terrifying, I asked Jesus why he took me to hell.

When I visited heaven and hell, I was only nine years old, so I had no clear conviction that heaven and hell was real. I wasn't sure of my salvation even though my dad was a pastor. Every evening at home, the whole family gathered together to worship with prayer and reading the Bible. We went to church every Sunday whether we wanted to or not. After worship, I would eat with other church members who came to church and we studied the Bible together, but I really did not have a clear confidence of heaven and hell.

While in heaven, Jesus spoke to me.

"This is your choice.
Will you believe in me and come to heaven, which is full of happiness and joy or will you go to hell with pain and suffering?
You have already seen heaven and hell."

He was right. The reason Jesus showed heaven and hell to me was to make sure that I had a clear understanding of it before I made the decision to trust in Him. How can I say that I would not choose the Kingdom of Heaven in this situation when I have already experienced heaven and hell? How can I say that I do not know Him and forsake Him? I firmly vowed in my mind that I would surely go back to heaven, and that when I return to this world, I will live by believing in Jesus alone. The Lord told me before I came back to this land.

"Believe only in me, worship me only.
Obey your mother and father and love your older sister."

And He also spoke the following important words:

"I know you will go back and sin because you are not here.
But when you do, confess your sins.
Then all your sins will be gone.
Because you believe in me."

He also shared some practical advice:

"If you go back to earth, you may live in a very small house.
You may also experience difficulties and pain.
Even your parents may cause you trouble.
But do not complain. Be thankful for your life."

After that, Jesus also gave me hope and comfort saying:

"Who will break you from me, though you live in a small house?

Who will separate you from me because of persecution?

You are my daughter. You are my princess.

There is a very big house in heaven for you.

Although there are those who torment you, do not hurt them,

but give me your heart.

Come first to me. Come and talk to me.

I will give you peace of mind.

If they continue to make your life difficult, let your parents know."

I was also told that while living in the world we should focus on Jesus. We need to depend on Him when there is trouble or harassment from friends and others.

At that moment God took my arm and told me.

"Are you ready to go down again?"

"God! I do not want to go down!"

I responded to God with such begging as if a newborn baby was desperately crying for his mother's milk. At that moment God again spoke to me tenderly.

"One day soon I will bring you back to heaven."

The Lord said finally.

"I will be with you. I will be in you. Now is the time to go down."

I did not want to come down to this world because heaven was so good.

So I begged the Lord fervently.

"Lord, I want to stay here. Please let me stay here."

"No. It is not your time yet. You are still young. I will come to pick you up again someday."

The Lord said goodbye for the last time.

"Now we have to part ways."

I was so sad to hear that! I was sad when I thought I had to leave heaven and return to this world. Of course I have a loving father, mother, sister and church friends on earth, but I really did not want to leave the heavens because I knew that the joy and happiness I had in heaven could not be compared with anything else on earth. If I could, I wanted to live with Jesus in heaven forever. There is no sadness or tears in heaven, no scolding, no homework, no examinations. Rather, it is full of true joy, happiness and satisfaction, and above all, you can live with God-your true father-and Jesus, who loves you forever.

Jesus said to me,

"Do not be disappointed; go down and be good and faithful."

While I was in heaven, I embraced God and Jesus five times.

Before the final separation, God hugged me.

Like the first time God took me to heaven, God grabbed my arms again and said.

"Are you ready to go down?"

Immediately God sent me down. At that time when I turned to see God, the face of God was still so bright that I could not look at his face properly. Soon I saw the door of heaven, and the door was very bright. With Him, my body came out of the door of heaven and came back to this land. When I came down to the ground again, the pure white dress I was wearing was gone, and I was wearing my purple shirt and pink pants while praying in church.

3. Crying a Lot

The prayer meeting was almost ending. When I got back from heaven, most of the children were done praying and sitting in small groups. I came back from heaven, and without realizing it, tears were constantly flowing from my eyes. A friend who was praying with me looked at me and said.

"I met God ..."

As soon as she said that, I started crying.

"God…"

As soon as I heard the word, my tears suddenly flowed like a waterfall, I could not control myself. I missed Jesus so much!

"God… Jesus…"

Just by calling or listening to, these names caused tears to flow down my cheeks.

At that time, a church teacher who heard our crying came to us saying,

"Ellen! Do you want to go home and see your mother?"

The teacher misunderstood and thought we were crying because we missed our moms.

"Not really. I saw Jesus in heaven…"

Tears flowed constantly, even the next day. I went to the bathroom to wash my face and cleaned my face with a tissue, but it did not stop the tears from flowing. During dinnertime, if I thought about Jesus, I could not eat because I would cry so much.

The next day we had communion. During the communion, I cried constantly. The Lord's Supper reminded me of Jesus' suffering on the cross for my sins. He had a simple meal with his disciples the night before he would suffer and be crucified. During the communion, I was thinking about the meal I had with Jesus in heaven. When I thought about that time, I wanted to see Jesus again, and I could stop the tears from flowing.

The next evening, the teachers held a ceremony to wash the children's feet. I remembered Jesus' feet I saw in heaven during the foot washing ceremony. I thought of the hole in Jesus' feet. Thinking about it, the tears that had stopped for a while began to flow again.

On the last day of the meeting, teachers and friends spent time writing a letter to God on a white sheet of paper and sending it off on a balloon. I wrote on my stationary that I really wanted to see Jesus and that I wanted to go back to heaven. I prayed earnestly to God in my heart.

"God. Look at this and take me back to heaven. I want to go back to heaven."

I heard God's voice clearly in my heart.

"Yes, I will pick you up again soon."

4. Living for Jesus

I am eleven years old. It has been about two years since I visited heaven. When my mom and dad decided to go to Thailand as missionaries through an international mission organization called WEC International, I had no idea where it was and what life would be like there. I just had a vague idea that

"I wanted to go to another country and have different experiences."

I did not think about separation from my grandparents and uncle or the many friends I had made in school and church. I just had a vague notion and expectation that it would be fun and exciting to live in a different country with my parents and sister.

When I arrived in Thailand I learned that they did not have a proper school for me to attend because it was a small rural area. If I wanted to go to school, like my older sister I would have to leave my mom and dad and stay at a place where I would have to take care of things all by myself at the age of eleven. I had no choice but to be home-schooled. It was very lonely because I did not have friends to play with or talk to.

I have loved people ever since I was small, so I always wanted to talk and play with people of any age without prejudice. In spite of my outgoing personality, there weren't many people in Tak whom I could play with and become friends with. There were occasional meetings with other missionaries, and occasionally visitor from other countries for a few days, but these encounters did not fill my lonely heart. I felt that these are the difficulties many missionary children have to suffer. As an eleven-year-old in the middle of my 5th grade in the United States, I had to leave my school and go to the mission field. In fact, when my family first arrived in Thailand, I did not think so much about my experience visiting heaven and hell. I was so busy trying to adapt to the unfamiliar environment in the mission field that I could not ponder those beautiful and joyous experiences in heaven. As I began to get used to life in an unfamiliar environment, I started to miss my friends and family in the United States. Moreover, when you are home-schooled alone in a new place, the homesickness grows. Whenever I get homesick, I sometimes think of my experiences in heaven.

God, who showed me the heavens when I was only nine years old, knew that I would encounter such a lonely and tough situation. He gave me the experience of seeing heaven to comfort me and give me hope. When I was lonely and stressed because I had no friends around me, I was reminded of the experience that I had with Jesus in heaven. Remembering these experiences gave me great strength. My mom and dad always said that to live for Jesus on earth is the most precious and beautiful way to live. My experiences in heaven made this real for me.

When I followed my parents during their ministry travels around Thailand, I saw many great temples, monks and idols. Especially as you go out of the city and into the countryside, you will see many temples and idols. The Thai people build a spirit house in a big building or in front of their house, and they put food there for the spirits every morning. Every time they go to and from home, they worship at the spirit house and ask the spirits to take good care of them. The idols in the houses of demons that they have built cannot walk or speak, but the Thai people live as though these idols would keep them safe and lead them to heaven.

Whenever I think about the Thai, I feel that I should let them know about Jesus whom I met in heaven. The fact that hell exists is so vivid and clear to me that it is an undeniable truth. Therefore, I realize that sharing the gospel of Jesus in this world, and preaching the precious heavenly gospel to the ends of the earth, is more important than anything else a Christian can do.

I want to give my life to this work.

Part 4.

A Seed Planted
for the Kingdom of God

1. A Sudden Calling

2. Hope for the Resurrection

3. A Seed of the Kingdom of God

4. What if ...

5. A Seed Begins to Bear the Fruit

6. Leaving Her Last Word

7. Saying Goodbye

8. Until We See You Again

Part 4. **A Seed Planted for The Kingdom of God**

1. A Sudden Calling

When we first went to Thailand, we had to stay in Chiang Mai for seven months. Then we had to move to another area according to the policy of WEC-Thailand. Out in the countryside of Tak and Khong Wilai, Ellen was alone without friends. We searched for a school that taught in English, but in that area, there was none. As a result, Ellen was home-schooled for two years and six months.

We, her parents became her teachers and we taught Ellen at home every day, but it was not easy. An eleven-year-old girl, cheerful and bright in nature and who likes to hang out with other people, found the isolation very difficult.

Nevertheless, being the optimistic child she was, she never lost her cheerful, outgoing personality and always had a smile on her face. After two and a half years of home schooling, when she was admitted to Grace International School in Chiang Mai. She was ecstatic! Grace International School is a school established to educate missionary children. For several reasons, she was not able to enter the dormitory operated by WEC Thailand, but was able to stay in another dormitory run by Korean missionaries. By entering boarding school in the eighth grade at the age of thirteen, she started a new life.

Ellen, who was born in America and lived only in the United States and Thailand, had some difficulties in understanding and adapting to the Korean language and culture in the Korean-run dormitory. However, thanks to the dedicated care of her dorm parents, she was able to adapt well. It was not long before she made lots of friends with her bright, friendly personality. After finishing her first semester, she came back to the Khong Wilia area to celebrate Christmas holidays with us. While she was with us, we had time every day to read and meditate on the Word of God in Genesis one of the Old Testament. During that short vacation, she prepared for her second semester.

After Ellen finished her three-week vacation, she went back to study in Chiang Mai, which is about five and a half hours by car, and the second semester of 2018 began. January 21st would be Ellen's birthday, so my wife and I went to surprise her a week early. We were also supposed to have family counseling for missionaries. My wife and I stayed in a guest room for missionaries not far from Ellen's dormitory.

She had not been informed beforehand, so she was delighted to hear that her parents had come up to Chiang Mai. Every day after school, she came to the guest room where we were staying and had dinner with us. After dinner, she would do her homework and we would have family worship. Later, she would return to her dorms and go to school the next day.

A few days, on Friday afternoon Ellen went with us for family counseling. After an hour of counseling, we went to a nearby restaurant to have a delicious meal. Suddenly, during the meal, Ellen said,

"Daddy! I love you!"

Usually, she would say,

"I like mom better than dad. Dad is…so so…"

She said this in such a serious manner that day, that it surprised me. I did not realize that it would be her last expression of love to me. After dinner, we went back to the guesthouse where we were staying and went to sleep peacefully.

The next day, she went to Saturday Korean School run by the nearby church and spent a pleasant Saturday afternoon with her friends. After that, she returned to the guesthouse and talked with us about what she wanted to do for her fourteenth birthday. After this pleasant conversation, she went to her room next to our room. Because it was Saturday, she did not have to return to her dorms. She enjoyed being able to with us for the weekend.

Until she went to bed, she had fun talking to her mom and she even talked to her older sister Rin in the USA. As sisters often talk to each other and share their thoughts and happenings; they talked for a while. Ellen's final message to her older sister to finish the conversation was,

"Unnie (means my older sister in Korean), I love you."

I never imagined that this conversation would be the last farewell to her sister. After saying goodbye, Ellen went to bed.

Sunday, January 14th at 1:30 A.M.

Suddenly, Ellen awoke from her sleep, clutched her hands to her chest and burst into our room next door complaining of pain.

"Dad! I can't breathe."

She cried,

"It's so hard to breathe!"

I was surprised out of my sleep, but because she had been suffering from asthma, I tried to stabilize her with the nebulizer. Generally, after administering the nebulizer about three times, she would return to normal as if nothing had happened, so we were not really concerned.

In this case however, my wife cried out, praying in tongues and drawing blood from Ellen's ten fingers and ten toes, but unfortunately there was no relief, and the symptoms kept getting worse. After calling for an ambulance, I prayed for Ellen and continued to use the nebulizer to restore her breathing. I tried urgently and made every effort to help her breathe again. However, contrary to our expectations, she gradually lost consciousness and the strength drained from her body. Only a few hours before, she had gone to bed with the color in her face. Now her face, which had been bright, turned purple in a matter of minutes. I was frantic because of the changing color of her face, so I could not stop trying to revive her. I kept trying and crying for my child's survival. Sadly, once her face turned purple, she did not regain consciousness. I tried to revive her with mouth-to-mouth resuscitation, but with no result. The effort to oxygenate Ellen's lungs through multiple artificial respirations was unfortunately not helping to restore her. In spite of my efforts she lost consciousness.

After 20 to 30 minutes an ambulance arrived and several emergency first-aid responders began to take steps to revive Ellen, who was lying in the room. Emergency personnel tried to wake her up with various emergency measures, including CPR, and as a last resort-using a stun gun-but she did not regain consciousness. When the emergency officials realized that her condition was too critical, they decided that it would be better to take her to the hospital. They took her in the ambulance and rushed her to the nearest emergency room.

Another emergency medical team, including the doctor in charge, who had been waiting for her at the hospital, continued to take emergency measures. Unfortunately, Ellen did not revive but took her last breath on earth. Because it was so sudden, for a long time, my wife and I could not believe what had just happened.

Just a few hours ago, Ellen had talked kindly to her mom and on the phone to her sister in the USA. Now, she was lying on the bed in the hospital emergency room!

It was an unbelievable situation for me and my wife. Whether Ellen knew our state of being, I do not know, but she did not look like a girl who had lost her life. Even though she was lying on a cold hospital bed, Ellen's face looked as if she were asleep. I thought that she would get up if I woke her. My wife shook her body several times and continued a one-sided conversation.

"Ellen, wake up! We have to go home!
Ellen, you can't keep sleeping here!
You have to go home and sleep!
Get up quickly!
Let's go home!
Let's go home!"

Without wiping all the tears that could not be controlled, we continued to try waking her up as if she were only sleeping. She did not respond to our calls or shaking of her body.

After confirming her death with the doctor, we stood blankly in the cold, morning air of the emergency room.

At dawn, after I called the leader of the WEC Thailand in Tak and the leader of the mission organization in the USA, I kept crying with tears that would not stop.

2. Hope for the Resurrection

While Ellen was staying with us for Christmas vacation in December back in 2017, a couple we had known well in the USA took a 20-hour flight to visit us on January 1st, 2018.

The Kangs own a private business in California, and he is the director of Disciple of Christ Fellowship (DCF-USA). This mission is raising up and training Korean American youths. Every year, they use their precious vacation time to visit the missionaries they have a relationship with and encourage them in their ministries. Instead of taking tours of a country, they counsel and encourage the hard-working missionaries. They pray for the missionaries fervently and continually.

Before they visited our home, Mr. Kang asked me if there was anything we wanted to have. At that time, Ellen asked for American snacks such likes Doritos, Sun Chips and American chocolate. After the long flight, the two of them finally arrived at our home in the rural area of Khong Wilai, bringing a bunch of sweets that Ellen had asked for. To my surprise, he packed up the full of these treats that were only available in the United States in a large suitcase. He opened the large suitcase on the spot and showed it to Ellen. As soon as she saw it, Ellen's eyes turned bright and she was very happy and joyful. She danced around and kept saying,

"Thank you! Thank you!"

This couple ate with Ellen, talked with her and had a really good time. They were worried about Ellen because they knew that she was being home-schooled in an isolated situation, but their arrival and witnessing of Ellen's bright demeanor put them at ease. They told me this later.

After spending about two days together with Ellen, we asked our field leader in Tak to take Ellen back to Chiang

Mai for her second semester studies. Back at home, we had time to share our concerns and difficulties on the mission field with this couple. They prayed for our ministry. They also shared a special theme and encouragement from the Word with us.

After sending Ellen back to Chiang Mai on the 3rd of January, we started Bible study with the Kangs and went till midnight. The next day, we started early in the morning and studied until one o'clock in the afternoon. It was a really refreshing time. The subject of the Bible study was the resurrection of Jesus Christ. In our Christian life, the Lord's death and resurrection is such an important truth to remember and place our hope in, that we cannot overlook it.

In particular, our Christian life does not end with death, which is not something to be afraid of or sad about. No matter what kind of death we experience on earth, we will surely be alive again after death— that is the promise of resurrection. After these Bible studies, I was re-affirmed in my conviction to follow the example of Jesus' disciples who went from Jerusalem, to Judea, Samaria and to the ends of the earth preaching and teaching the death and resurrection of Jesus.

The disciples who followed Jesus for three years, only to see Him dying on the cross, and were disappointed and discouraged that they denied Him as their teacher and ran away. But after seeing that Jesus had been resurrected on the third day after His death, their lives were completely transformed. They believed that after death in this world, there would be a resurrection to eternal life just like that of Jesus. Through the resurrection event, it became clear to them that Jesus was the only Way, Truth and Life.

The disciples became convinced that the resurrection of Jesus after three days in the tomb, was clear evidence that God is alive and powerful. At the same time, it became clear and that Jesus is the true God that all the people in this world must believe in, and that the resurrected Jesus must be both Savior and Lord of all the living and the dead.

Therefore, in the extreme situations of suffering, and even loss of life here on this earth, we have to boldly proclaim the gospel. When I considered the situation of the Thai people who did not know or believe in Jesus, I became very sad.

In this spiritually dark land, with no hope for heaven, but with a vague fear of the curse of many demons, hell is closer to them than heaven. I was once again convinced that the truth of the resurrection, which gives life and hope, is a vital part of my ministry.

After sharing such a valuable Bible study with us, Mr. Kang and his wife— having no time to tour Thailand— returned to the States. Ten days after they left Thailand, they suddenly heard the news of the death of Ellen, and they were shocked. Ellen, the bright and cheerful girl, whom they had seen only ten days earlier, was now called by God and no longer exists in this world. It was shocking to think that they would not see her again on this earth.

The heartache of parents who lose their beloved child cannot be eased by anything. What gave us much comfort and encouragement was God's Word that confirmed to us the hope and reality of the resurrection that will come after the death of the flesh.

After the funeral, realizing that we will not see Ellen in this world again, we shed many tears. Nevertheless, our heart was not filled with despair, frustration, or discouragement. Rather, we were filled with comfort, a courageous expectation and hope to meet with Ellen in heaven soon.

3. Becoming a Seed of the Kingdom of God

The dawn of the Lord's Day when Ellen was called to heaven.

Leaving her cold body alone in the hospital morgue, I called the US consulate in Chiang Mai before dawn. Because it was early on Sunday morning, I could not speak to the consul in person. Instead, I left a message with the assistant that my daughter, a US citizen, was called to heaven.

A few hours later, the US consul in Chiang Mai called me back. First, she expressed her sincere condolences in regard to the death of our child, and explained that since

Ellen was an American citizen, they can help in many ways concerning the whole process of laying her to rest. In addition to helping to resolve various legal issues in dealing with the Thai authorities, they could specifically assist in transferring the body to New York. The consul, who spoke directly with me, was very kind and told me in detail what procedures are in place for Americans who lose their lives in a foreign country.

Before Ellen's body was placed in to the coffin, while she was sleeping alone in the morgue, I had to inform her mother, Ihnyoung, of this information and discuss where to take Ellen's body. We talked about whether or not we would like to bury her in New York near her grandmother and grandfather, who loved her very much.

When I shared what the American consul said, Ellen's mother, Ihnyoung— despite the offer of the positive help of the US consul—said,

"If we take Ellen's body to the United States and bury Ellen there,
I don't think we can come back to the land of

Thailand. I cannot leave
my daughter's body alone in America and come back
here to minister."

I was sympathetic to her belief that if we took Ellen's body and buried her in New York, we would never have the courage or confidence to return to this land of Thailand. While we were having this conversation, God put an amazing thought in my heart. To my astonishment, I realized that the Lord wants Ellen to be planted as

'A Seed of the Kingdom of God for Thailand'

I was absolutely sure that the thought that Ellen was the seed of heaven chosen by the Lord for the Thai was not my own idea. At the same time, the thought God put into my heart came back repeatedly as a strong conviction. While we were living comfortably in the States, God stirred our heart to follow His leading, so He could bring us all to this land to share the gospel. It was clearly God's leading and calling, so even in this difficult situation, God's great desire is for our ministry to continue here in Thailand. This conviction became more and more clear as time went by.

A young 13-years-old.

Like a flower that did not have a chance to bloom, the Lord seemingly took our beloved Ellen too soon. Still, the Lord knows and loves Ellen even more than her parents do. He who has guided every journey of our family so far, will continue to go before us. We know that He is good and that He is always preparing us what is ahead. Though the tragedy tore our hearts and we could not understand what happening before us, the Lord always prepares good things for us. He is always good!

Yes!
God is Good! All the Time!

The death of Ellen is not easy to bear, but we believed in the goodness and faithfulness of the Lord, who works everything together for good. The Lord helped us make the decision to bury Ellen's body in Tak, in the middle of Thailand.

After we decided to bury our child in Thailand, we called back to the US Consulate in Chiang Mai and informed them of our decision. The consul responded that she respected our decision. She spoke kindly and told me in detail which documents that I would need to finalize the process, then she hung up.

After this conversation, I discussed with the missionaries the specific details of what it would take to move Ellen to Tak to bury her. First, we would need a coffin and then transportation to move her. After these preparations, several WEC missionaries ministering in Chiang Mai and Chiang-Mai Mission Church, went to prepare for the funeral. On behalf of us, a sad and grieving couple, they arranged for all the funeral schedules and procedures in Chiang Mai. In the afternoon of the Lord's Day, the funeral of our beloved Ellen began with the Entrance Worship service in Chiang Mai.

We were preparing for a three-day funeral, but two days in the hospital morgue in Chiang Mai and three days in the church in Kamphengphet, made it a five-day funeral. Many missionaries, local church members in Thailand, and Grace International School officials came together to comfort and encourage us. During these five days of the funeral, a memorial service was offered every evening. Some of the people who attended the service made encouraging comments like this:

> "The sorrow of losing Ellen is so big and painful, it
> is hard to bear,
> but this funeral service has been so comforting and
> graceful!"

Although He is the God who took Ellen early in her life, He was with us in this funeral and gracious in guiding the whole process. A few weeks after the funeral, we went to Korea to extend our first daughter, Rin's visa and met certain people who heard the sad news about Ellen. They said that the death of this child, and the fact that Ellen's body is buried on the mission field of Thailand, especially the Tak area, has a very special meaning.

They said that Ellen had already been taken to heaven at the age of nine and had experienced the Kingdom of Heaven. She came to this country of Thailand, with the seeds of heaven already planted in her body and soul, and the seed planted in that soul were now dead. Her body is buried in the land of Thailand, and in fact, God has made it like a channel, which is like a shining light linking the heavenly world and the earthly world— a connection between a world full of light and a world full of darkness.

They explain it again to us. In particular, the death of a missionary on a mission field is not merely a normal death, but a martyr's death and it plays an important role in conveying the light of truth about heaven to a land full of darkness. Our role as missionaries is to proclaim the light and life of heaven to those on this earth. God revealed to me that the death of our daughter had an important significance, just as that of the disciples of Jesus, who had spread the gospel all over the world and brought the light of heaven to the earth by virtue of living, dying and being in as martyrs in those places.

These friends in Korea comforted us by saying that because Ellen's body was buried in Thailand instead of the U.S., it would play a very important role in opening the amazing purpose of the Lord in Thailand. They saw clearly that Ellen has become the seed of heaven that connects the heavenly world filled with light and the earthly world filled with darkness. They encouraged and prayed with us and reminded us that it is not by our own strength or endeavor, but that God would bear fruit from this precious seed.

I am reminded that when the first missionaries came to the land of Joseon (old Korea) with the Gospel, they went through much persecution and oppression. Those missionaries and children could have returned to their homelands when it became difficult or when they encountered diseases. However, through their devotion to the spiritually deprived land of the former Joseon(old Korea), they eventually revealed the light of the gospel to the spiritually dark land of Korea.

This precious dedication of Ellen, who has been offered as a sacrifice for the benefit of the Thai people. Her martyrdom plants the seed of heaven in Thailand, where the atmosphere is that of a spiritually barren and wilderness similar to the early Joseon period in Korea. It is a precious gift of God to use our daughter's death to extend the Kingdom of God. They said that they are sure God will use it as a tool of His own.

After few days later, a missionary couple who could not attend Ellen's funeral wanted to visit Ellen's gravesite. When we took them to the cemetery, the missionary, praying in front of Ellen's headstone, made a very meaningful statement about Ellen's death. Ellen 's tomb is located in a small cemetery for local Thai Christians. We felt thankful that the cemetery where we buried Ellen was in our ministry area of Tak. However, a fact we learned after Ellen's funeral was that there was a memorial marker of a foreign couple about 4-5 meters to the left of Ellen's grave.

We found out that those-laid to rest here-were the first missionaries sent to WEC Thailand from WEC-USA. They were sent from America just like our family. Their names were Wilfred and Evelyn Overgaard. The first time they came to Thailand was in 1947, and they faithfully served until 1974. Then they retired and returned to the State, where they spent the rest of their live. Before they died, they asked their children to bury their remains in Thailand. The graves next to Ellen's were theirs.

Later, when we had a chance to come to the US and

review the history of WEC- Thailand again, we discovered an interesting coincidence. It was not just these two missionaries who came to Thailand in the name of WEC with the gospel at the beginning. Wilfred and Evelyn Overgaard came with their two young children, Paul and Sharon. Two single ladies came with them. Their names were Fern Berg and Ellen Gillman.

I was really surprised to learn about this, especially in significant detail.

Of course it can be considered a coincidence, but it was amazing to discover that the name of an early single missionary who came to Thailand was Ellen, the same name as that of our daughter. The meaning of Ellen in Hebrew is grace, mercy and light of God.

Anyway, through the prayers of the missionary couple who visited Ellen's gravesite, God spoke spiritually meaningful words to our hearts. It was a great comfort and encouragement to us who had our beloved child buried in this land of Thailand.

According to this couple, WEC missionaries began the work in Thailand in 1947, so the 70th anniversary has passed. The year of Ellen's death was the 71st year of WEC ministry in this land, and it represents the beginning of a new time of harvest. Ellen has become a child-martyr-her life laid down for the sake of the Gospel in Thailand-and this is a sign that the Lord has special purposes to fulfill and amazing things to accomplish through her death.

In the history of Israel, it was during the seventy years after Judah and Northern Israel had been destroyed and taken captive to Babylon, that the Israelites experienced many years of pain and hardship. WEC-Thailand also went through much toil and many difficulties during the first 70 years of missionary work. But now, with the beautiful, heavenly seed of this child planted, hope and expectation abound for life and truth to spring out of death and bring many Thai into the kingdom of God.

The fact that Ellen went to heaven on January 14th also has a very important meaning. In the history books of the Bible, we see that after 430 years of slavery in Egypt, the Israelites experienced the first Passover and the Exodus, led by Moses. The first celebration of the Passover took place at a designated time on the Jewish calendar year. It was to begin on January 14th and ends on January 21st. I think it is more than a coincidence that Ellen was called to heaven on January 14th and her 14th birthday is January 21st.

In this way, Ellen's life and death are aligned with the historical record of the Bible, the first year after 70 years of captivity, and the first day of the Passover, a week-long celebration.

Surprisingly, all of these times were precisely matched as if someone was intentionally planning it. In addition, all her life and death were related to the number 7, which is the number that signifies completion in the Bible. As they shared these words with us, the missionary and his wife comforted us by saying,

> "Let us give thanks to the Lord because He planned Ellen's life and death and used Ellen as a tool for preparing the expansion of the Kingdom of God in Thailand."

When we see many people being born and dying in the world, sometimes it is sadly deplorable and meaningless in sadness. But knowing that the Lord is using Ellen's death as an important seed for the Kingdom of God in Thailand is cause for true thankfulness.

4. What If ...

During the five-day funeral service, there was nothing that we could do. We could only bear the sadness and the tears that flowed down our faces. Suddenly, this questioning thought passed through my mind:

What if...?
What if...Ellen had not been sent to Chiang Mai and had just stayed at Khong Wilai with us?

What if...we had just sent her to live with her grandmother in the United State she has asked?

What if... we did not come here to become missionaries, but stayed in America?

And what if ...the Lord had not called our family to be missionaries?

What if ...? What if ...? What if ...?

At the end of all these questioning thoughts came a spirit of bitterness toward God.

I questioned and accused Him because this tragedy concerning my beloved youngest daughter was so devastating. My heart was filled with the overwhelming question,

"Why?"
"You had to take a little girl so early! Why?"

"Why did this kind of sadness come to our family!"

We obeyed you and went whenever and wherever you wanted us to go.

"Why did you lead us like this?"

"Why did you give us such trials, hardships and pain?"

More negative thoughts flood my mind:

"She has not even seen grandmothers, grandfathers and uncles in the United States!"

"Our older daughter, Rin, has been studying in the United States, and she has not seen Ellen for two years!"

These negative thoughts continued to come.

But suddenly I realized that this attitude of bitterness and complaining is not something God would want, rather something that would make the devil clap his hands.

That's right.

For Christians who follow the Lord, difficulties and

adversity sometimes come at unexpected times and with unwelcome circumstances, but in the pain and suffering of life, we still need to trust the Lord who guides and guards us without our even realizing it. We need to respond to Him with gratitude rather than holding grudges and complaining. I realized in the midst of my sorrow that this is a confession of faith that the Lord greatly desires us to firmly declare. The response of thankfulness and praise in the midst of trouble time needs to be more than just a belief in the mind. It needs to be a way of life.

With this revelation, we started looking for areas of gratitude rather than being disappointed with God. When we started searching for reasons to be grateful, we found that there were many things to be thankful for. Among the many things of thanksgiving, a typical thanks from the last funeral service were as follows:

First, we thanked God for sending Ellen as a gift of God to us for 13 years.

Second, we thanked God that when she was nine years old, Ellen experienced heaven and hell, and met Jesus, and now she is in the arms of Jesus who loves her.

Third, we were thankful that Ellen would become a seed of Kingdom of God for the lost soul of Thailand.

Fourth, those who do not know Jesus have to live with uncertainty of their afterlife, but we knew that after this life, we will surely meet Ellen again.

After the funeral, we placed a small monument over Ellen's grave in Tak.

On the tombstone there is a picture of Ellen and the following words:

'A Seed of the Kingdom of God for Thailand'

A seed of the Kingdom of God for Thailand

Ellen Eun Her

1.21.2004 – 1.14.2018

사랑스런 아이
주의 품에 안기다

Beloved child of God embraced in His Arms

5. A Seed Begins to Bear the Fruit

We have heard from many people the amazing stories of how Ellen's death, and the planting of her as the seed of heaven for Thailand, has been concretely bearing fruit.

There is a Thai woman living a faithful life in the Khong Wilai church where we worked for a while. Her son K, the second of her three children, did not go to the high school, but did drugs and hung out with friends around the neighborhood. His wayward life was enough to bring worry and concern not only of his mother, but also many people who knew him. Therefore, one of the most important prayer topics of this woman was the conversion of K and transformation of his life. We visited him in order to evangelize and share the gospel with him. We also invited him many times to study God's Word and come to church, but every time we asked, K not only refused our request but also showed no interest in God or the church.

Amazingly, the week after the funeral, K 's mother came to us with excitement and informed my wife saying,

> "Ajan (Thai words when calling a missionary or pastor)!
> K has decided to come to church next week!"

When K who had been ignoring our invitations to go to the church attended Ellen's funeral and said that he would go to church, even though I did not ask him-we were overjoyed. I was amazed and happy, and said,

"Praise the Lord!"

At the time when I heard this news, my heart, which was burdened with the death of our beloved Ellen, started to slowly soften. When I went to church the next Lord's Day, I was surprised to see that K was seated next to his mother, ready to worship.

"K! Nice to see you. Have you decided to come to church?"

"Yes. I will be coming to church every Sunday."

"Then please come to study God's Word with Ajan."

"Yes, I understand. I will try hard to learn the Bible."

It was a brief conversation, but I could hear a softness in his voice as he responded to my suggestion of studying the Bible. Then, as I promised, we started Bible study with

K. During one of our Bible study time, I asked him what caused him to return to church. He said,

"I attended the funeral with my mother on the last morning of Ellen's funeral, without any serious thought, but in the midst of the funeral service, my heart told me strongly that I need to go to church."

"Even now I cannot explain how my hard and rough heart became so soft. My heart was cold like the ice, hard floor in the wintertime, but at Ellen's funeral, it melted as if spring had arrived. I had a strong urge to go back to church."

We were very surprised at the change that had placed in K when we met him again at church, and we thanked God for working in his heart and mind. The death of our daughter was the seed of heaven for Thailand, just as the Lord had said, and K became the first fruit in Thailand.

The death of a 13-year-old child may seem insignificant, but the Lord began to bear fruit on this earth through it. After returning home from the funeral, we had to sort out the rest of the things that were left behind in Chiang Mai where Ellen had been in school in order to return to our mission field in Khong Wilai. As the three of us went up to Chiang Mai in the car together, when we looked back, the empty space for Ellen in the car made our hearts hurt even harder. With wounded heart, our family headed for Chiang Mai to clean up the last traces of our beloved daughter.

After five and a half hours of long driving, we finally arrived at the dormitory where Ellen had lived. Before retrieving the items from Ellen's room, we talked to Korean missionary couple that was in charge of the dorms. The two of them were very shocked by the sudden death of Ellen, and the sisters and brothers who lived with Ellen were also having trouble with the thought of her death.

However, when my family met with both missionaries in Chiang Mai and the students who were in Ellen's dorm, we were comforted by the fact that God had been touching their hearts and that they were recovering gradually through the process of professional psychological counseling. Through meeting together, we comforted each other's pain and had time to pray together for the Lord to heal us all.

The day after retrieving her belongings from the dormitory we visited Grace International School. We could see God's goodness working at the school when we went to return the rest of her books and say thank you to the teachers and other staff.

The week after Ellen's funeral, the school had set up Spiritual Emphasis Week and students attended numbers of special seminars, discussions and prayer meetings.

Grace International School was established about ten years ago for the education of missionary children in Chiang Mai, northern Thailand. Because it is a school set up for such a special purpose, most of the students at this school are missionary kids as MKs. The students' parents are missionaries working mainly in Asia, Southeast Asia, the Middle East and even Africa. It is a valuable educational institution in Chiang Mai, Thailand, which is called the mission hub region of Southeast Asia. It is the ideal place for the education of missionary children whose parents work in remote areas where they cannot access standard education.

Most teachers and staff who work and serve at the school are missionaries who have been sent from all over the world. The teachers and staff who work here are dedicated people who also have a vision for the gospel to prosper in this part of the world. They are also missionaries in teaching the missionary kids both academically and spiritually.

We recently met a professional counselor who worked at the school for many years but we were shocked at her testimony. According to the counselor's observations over the years, most of the students in this school were missionary kids, but about 80% of them were nominal Christians who had little to no spiritual encounter with God. These spiritual realities were the counselor's biggest concern and caused her to pray for the students. She said that after Ellen's death, amazing things started happening in school.

During the Spiritual Emphasis Week after the funeral, many students visited their teachers and counselor and confessed their sins. They began to repent and resolved to live a life that was glorifying to God. When the students thought about Ellen who died at such an early age, they realized that it could happen to them also. When they faced such a sudden death, serious anxieties arose about going into heaven and seeing the Lord or falling helplessly into hell, and as a result, they started repenting.

Although they were Missionary Kids like Ellen and had left their familiar country at a young age with their parents, whether they wanted or not, Ellen's death became a personal challenge to their faith. Students facing such challenges now reached a spiritual turning point where they understood they must be accountable for their own lives.

In addition, a precious opportunity to examine their habitual and formal beliefs took place through Ellen's death. Since Grace International School was founded no student who attended this school had died suddenly. Because of this, the death of Ellen really caused a great shock and a deep sadness. It had a sobering effect on those students who were just exercising their spiritual routines out of habit or and to-meet-expectations. As a result, repentance and spiritual awakening arose among those students.

Many teachers talked about the spiritual awakening that took place at the school during Spiritual Emphasis Week. They attributed it to Ellen's death and its call for repentance and spiritual renewal.

In addition to the conversion of K, God was bearing fruit through Ellen's death in its impact upon the many missionary kids.

Ellen went to the Grace International School, in the eighth grade, but unfortunately only for one semester, before going to be with the Lord. The school returned tuition fees for the remaining semester. It was not that much money, but we started to pray about how to use the money in a meaningful way. It was only a small sum, so it would disappear without much meaning if we just used for everyday needs. We started to pray and ask God how it could be used most effectively for His kingdom.

The idea that the Lord gave us at that time was to use the money to serve the middle and high school students in Thailand. In particular, it was to select a few from among the church's hard-working students who were poor and unable to pay for tuition. Then we would create an agency that could specifically help those Thai children.

Though it was not a large sum of money, I want to make a scholarship foundation using this money as seed money. Because it was money that should be used for a good cause, I started the Ellen Her Foundation to provide continuing support for Thai students who needed financial aid to attend school.

The Bible tells of a time when Jesus preached in the countryside of Bethsaida, many people were hungry because they had been there all day with nothing to eat, the Lord fed the multitudes through blessing of the five small loaves and two little fish.

If, like the miracle of the five loaves and two fish, though the money we have given is small, it is blessed in the Lord's hands, I hope that through this money many students in the land of Thailand will grow up beautifully as God's people. When I shared these thoughts with a few missionaries, they encouraged me saying that it was a very good idea, and they kindly advised me and helped with the scholarship project specifically. I am expectant that God will do good and beautiful work in this ministry that will help the Thai students grow to become leaders in the church and their country. The specific plans for this scholarship fund were formulated through prayer, and as a result, we have already selected several students and families and started to donate a small amount of scholarship money every month together with intercessory prayer for them. I hope to see the students receiving this assistance as future workers for God in Thailand.

One family chosen to receive the scholarship wept in front of us as soon as they heard this news. They shared their story that they faced many troubles due to their child's school expenses. When they heard about the scholarship, they thanked the Lord for answering their prayers. When I first met this family, I was very surprised and confused, but I realized that the project of helping Thai students by establishing this kind of scholarship foundation was not ours but that it came from God. Although I cannot see my beloved daughter anymore on earth, I pray that many more second and third "Ellens" will appear throughout Thailand in the future. I also hope to see many students receiving this scholarship, to be raised as God 's precious workers for the land of Thailand in the future.

In order to attend the funeral, Ellen's sister, Rin took a leave of absence from her university in the States. When we were finished with the funeral and took care of all the other activities related to Ellen's death, we realized that a month had passed. When Rin entered Thailand suddenly from the United States, she came in with a Tourist Visa, which allows one to stay in Thailand for 30 days only. Now she had to travel to another country to renew her visa.

We rushed to Korea, where we met many supporters who had heard the sad news about Ellen. The comfort and encouragement of many of those whom we met strengthened us in our resolve. At the same time, they expressed disappointment in hearing about the present challenges of Christian missions in Thailand, where more than 90 % of the people are Buddhists. In Thailand, Buddhism is the official state religion. Around 7 to 8% are believed to be Muslims, especially in Phuket, a southern region well-known for tourism and vacation destinations. There are a few minority groups scattered mainly in the mountains around Chiang Mai and Chiang Rai provinces in the north, who believe in Christ, including Catholics, who are found mainly in central Bangkok.

Over the past 190 years, a number of ministries had been established by mission organizations, but the rate of Christian evangelization today is not even 1%. Despite the long history of Christian missions, those who evaluate the progress of the Gospel still classify Thailand, especially the Thai majority, as unreached peoples who desperately need evangelism. In spite of the sacrifice and dedication of many missionaries, the evangelization rate is very low, and what we have personally realized is that the educational structure of Thailand is an important factor in this statistic.

Thailand has one of the best standards of living among the countries of the Indochina Peninsula. Compared to many other countries around the world, social infrastructures such as public facilities and medical care and education are considered well-established. In Thailand, people can send their child to kindergarten when the child is three years old or older. When they go to a kindergarten in the public schools, they have to learn to bow every morning and evening to Buddhist statues placed in each classroom. The children must learn Buddhist scriptures and doctrines whether they want or not.

Apart from public schools, there are many temples in Thailand that run primary school courses. Buddhist education in a temple is to be expected but it is also a normal part of life in the public and private schools in Thailand. Therefore, children grow up with Buddhist thoughts and values starting at an early age.

This Buddhist education is carried out throughout the entire elementary, middle and high school years before students go to university. In other words, the teaching and training on Buddhism, which starts from kindergarten, is strengthened through elementary, middle and high school years. After graduating from high school and college, Thai youth, usually become people who have impact on Thai society by their Buddhist values and ideas.

When the first missionaries came to Thailand to preach the gospel, they began to establish hospitals and were mainly involved in medical ministries, and thus began to influence the Thai society with the Gospel. In contrast, missions through education were relatively insignificant. After several decades, missionaries became interested in establishing Christian schools because of the need for a Christian influence through education, but most schools are located in Bangkok, the capital of Thailand, or Chiang Mai where most of the foreign population is concentrated. In the outskirts of the capital, other major metropolitan areas, or in small and medium-sized cities, few schools offer Christian-based education.

When we shared these spiritual realities about Thailand with our friends and acquaintances in Korea, some expressed a desire to educate Thai children in God's Word and the Gospel for effective and long-term evangelization. We did not even think about setting up a school in Thailand when we left that country in haste to renew our daughter's visa, but as we continued to meet people who were interested in establishing a Christian school, the project became a goal to be achieved.

Surprisingly, these conversations grew more fruitful and the possibility of establishing a school became a reality far beyond our expectations. The conversation about evangelization in Thailand, initiated by our setting up of Ellen Her Foundation, continued to grow into specific goals to set up a Christian organization to educate the children of Thailand.

Taking the plan one step further, we discussed concrete methods for Christian evangelization through public channels such as Christian schools and educational institutions. Our plan is to instruct Thai children in the Word and with Christian values starting at an early age so that when they grow up, they will become leaders of their country and influence the society with Christian values to expand the Kingdom of God. These schools would be bilingual, teaching Thai children English along with other subjects, as this is the common language among Southeast Asian countries especially in ASEAN (Association of Southeast Asian Nations).

It was agreed that a dozen of our prayer supporters would actively participate in the ministry plan. As a result, we started practical preparations for the establishment of a bilingual Christian school in Thailand under the Ellen Her

Foundation, and we are preparing to develop a Christian educational institution in Thailand. We are praying and hoping for an organization that lasts not only a generation after my wife and I leave this world, but for at least three generations up to 100 years of influencing and generating leaders for the country.

The Lord's words that our loving Ellen would be planted as the seed of the Kingdom of God for Thailand began to bear fruit surprisingly, though we did not expect it at all. Beginning with the conversion of a local child in Thailand, the repentance and renewal amongst the students at Grace International School, and the establishment of Ellen Her Foundation to help Thai students materially and spiritually, we see that the fruit of the seed is multiplying by leaps and bounds.

If a kernel of wheat does not fall and die on the ground, it will remain the same, but Jesus himself died as a grain of wheat and became fruitful. The outcome of His death and resurrection was that his twelves disciples became fruitful then 70 evangelists, and 120 people in Mark's attic were added to bear more fruit. About 2,000 years ago, the seed of the heaven planted through the sacrifice of Jesus on the cross. His death became the seed of life, because through it He conquered the power of sin and death. Today millions of people in many parts of the world are putting their hope in Him.

This all began with the death of a young, weak child who was only 13 years old, but through the death of this precious martyr, I hope to see the Lord glorify the fruit of heaven in this land of Thailand. When we think of things that have been done so far and see the visions for many ministries come forth, we confess that this is not our work, but God's work. When it is God's vision, it will bear fruit. We have a clear understanding of the fact that all of this is outside of our abilities, because we have no possibility of doing it on our own. We have no human network, and no foundational resources for ministry.

From the moment we first entered the mission field-from learning the language, to discipling and serving the Thai people-our knowledge and abilities were too limited. We knew that we were but weak, imperfect and incompetent servants. We confess that today we are only witnessing

God doing His work through us. This is not just our own vision regarding the scholarship foundation and a Christian educational institution in Thailand, but we have a clear conviction that the Lord is in it, and He will bring it to pass. We are simply praying and waiting for it to happen according to the Lord's timetable. At this point we can only silently watch how the Lord will accomplish these amazing things.

I am still pained when I think that I am not able to see Ellen again in this world, and I miss her terribly. Nevertheless, we thank our beloved Lord who brings fruit by His word and has called us to be missionaries to the Thai people. May He be exalted and glorified forever!

Logo for Ellen Her Foundation established in 2018

6. Leaving Her Last Word

During Christmas break when we were staying in Khong Wilai, before Ellen was called to heaven, we spent the evenings meditating on passage in the Bible.

At the young age of thirteen, when she went to live in the dorms at Chiang Mai, Ellen felt unsettled and struggled to get acclimated to her strange new environment. We realized that it was difficult for her to adjust and we tried to focus our Bible studies on passage that would comfort and encourage her in her difficulties.

Not only had Ellen met the Lord through her sudden experience of heaven and hell, but when she was a child, she strangely learned through experiences certain things that would happen in the future, much like Joseph.

Recognizing the similarities of Ellen's and Joseph's dream-guided lives, we focused our Bible study and meditation on the life of Joseph. Each day we shared with her how God guided and trained Joseph, and finally how He blessed and used him as a blessing the nation of Israel. Our sharing of these words became a great encouragement and comfort to Ellen, who was worn out from her school life.

Although there were hardships, loneliness and sometimes tears in her new environment, through such a process, the Lord would equip Ellen to live a more trusting and thankful life. Expecting the Lord to guide her to spiritual maturity, we encouraged her to grow in trusting and depending fully upon the Lord. When she was homeschooling with us, she was an immature young girl but we noticed changes in her mental and emotional growth just in the six months she spent at Chiang Mai.

Although not fully mature, we could see that our youngest child was gradually growing into a teenage girl. After about two weeks of sharing time with us, she returned to Chiang Mai and would frequently share in her Facebook post that:

"I'll be a better person. I will only trust in God."

She wanted to train her heart and mind to depend only on

the Lord until she went to heaven. God so prepared her to love and trust only in Him that her Facebook posts-the last words she left on earth-express her resolve to live a life trusting and depending upon the Lord.

Even when she may not have many friends around her, or when she encountered psychological and physical difficulties and hardships, Ellen was determined to become a child with whom God would be pleased. Trusting only in God in every situation should be the goal of all Christians who believe in Jesus. A person who allows God to change him or her becomes more beautiful in the sight of the Lord. Learning to trust in God alone helps us to persevere in any difficulties or adversities that we face. Considering that it is the Father's heart that we desire, we have learned that the short, last confession of Ellen is not merely a confession for herself but a challenge for all of us who live in this world. Although she was young, Ellen's last words posted on Facebook are a beautiful confession of her faith.

7. Saying Goodbye

On Thursday, when Ellen's funeral was finished at Tak, Grace International School hosted a memorial service to mourn the death of Ellen. For the students and teachers who could not attend the funeral ceremony held at Kampengphet, the school arranged a table in the school hall and many friends and teachers who knew Ellen wrote notes to say goodbye.

I would like to share some of these letters and notes that the school sent us.

Dear Ellen,

My dear,

You were a great blessing to me.

It was a blessing that I met you and knew you.

Thank you so much for being part of my life.

You will always be in my heart until we meet again.

Every time I saw you, you rushed to me and held my hands

and gave me a hug.

We will miss you a lot.

There were so many things I wanted to do together...
...using Cold stone coupons,
...getting our nails done,
...eating tasty food,
...drinking Ellen's special latte at Starbucks,
...teaching worship dance to the children,
...having a birthday party

I guess God loved Ellen too much.

When we meet later, show me the dance you've thought up...

I have learned so much from you.

I will continue to share your love with others.

Thank you for giving me a chance to look back and

think about my life again.

I am going to fight fiercely in the place

where God sends me and hold on to God more firmly.

Please watch over me.

Thank you for being a special gift to me.

When we meet again,

let's greet each other in our usual way.

My beautiful girl...

I love you very much.

Sister, M

My beloved Ellen,

You were the sunshine of my life.

You've always had a heart of encouragement and love.

I should have said this a little sooner ...

I love you.

You always made many people comfortable with your hugs.

You always knew how to make me smile even in my saddest days.

I still remember the first time we met

and introduced each other and shared our school schedule.

I hoped that 2018 would be

a time of many changes in your life as you wanted.

I am so grateful for your blessings and love for those

around you.

Thank you for staying true to yourself.
I love you.
Ellen.

Your life has given me a great encouragement.

I love you.

A

Dear Ellen,

The library is a dark place this week.

You aren't there.

After your death on Sunday,

a beautiful light left our book space.

Thank you for the joy and open spirit you brought.

I loved your kind words, your random questions,

your dreams, your laughter.

I wish I could watch you grow up and achieve your dreams.

I wish I could help you pick out another book,

or tell you to be quiet in the library.

I know you are now in the perfect arms of our perfect Savior,

and I hope you get to meet my young best friend Jonny.

He was your age.

He could tell you stories about our silly, beautiful friendship.

But I wish you were here.

It doesn't seem fair your life ended so soon -

but you, I'm sure, have A HUGE, PERFECT perspective on that.

You blessed me with your words, laughter and smile.

Thank you for sharing your life freely.

I wish I'd told you this all in person.

I'll tell you someday.

Your sad - for now

Mr. S.

When our family went to live in Chiang Mai for the first few days as missionaries, we stayed in a guest house for missionaries in the World Club. It turned out that this was the room that Ellen occupied the last time she was in Chiang Mai.

S, the last missionary to see Ellen, sent a short letter.

To beloved Ellen,
the last letter for you in this world…

You always said…

When I first saw you,
even when I last saw you.
You always said,

'I want to help you.'

When you first came here in Chiang Mai,
I could tell you
how lovely and pretty you were
when you expressed your pretty heart with a little bit
of Korean.

The sad and painful reality
that we cannot see you again in this world is
unbearable ...
We just do not know what to do.

Ellen!
Lovely Ellen ...

We are comforted by the fact that the heaven you
are in
is a much better place than this world.
There is no asthma, pain, sorrow where you are.
We are comforted by this truth.
I know that you are in the Lord's heaven,
but the separation in this land is heartbreaking and
sad ...

We will meet again in the near future ...
On that day when the Lord called ...
So the words that I didn't get to share in this world,
I want to ...
I would like to ask the Lord why he took you so early.

Ellen!

I love you ...
I miss you ...
and I'm sorry ...

I am really sorry that I did not know about your asthma
and that I did not pray enough for you ...

Goodbye Ellen ...
Let's meet again soon.
With gladness and joy ...

I love you,
I love you,
I love you,

Ellen ...

Missionary S.

There is a family in America who intercedes for us in prayer. These precious believers in the United States also remembered Ellen, and they sent us a letter to comfort us.

We can only imagine your heartache.
Our heart aches with you.

How much do you want to see your lovely Ellen.
Still,
when I was thinking of Ellen in the subway coming
home, she seemed to be comforting me by saying.

> *'Aunt, I am in heaven.*
> *Do not be sad.'*

I will await the day
when I will meet Ellen again with the resurrected
Lord.

We pray that you will hold on to the supernatural
peace of our Lord at this time of unbelievable grief.

Please tell us if there is anything we can do to help.

I do not think there is anything more painful than
the sadness of losing a child.
Only God the Father who sacrificed His only beloved
son and saved us seems to be able to comfort you.

Please remove the gate of the enemy
from the land where your daughter is buried.

Love the souls of that land
so that the death of your beloved Ellen is not in vain.

We look forward to the day
when the Thai people will wear white clothes
and stand with Ellen and you before the Lord.

We will also place Ellen in our hearts
and pray for Thailand and our two missionaries.
Missionary Hers.
I pray that the Lord will continue to be with you and
comfort you.

I believe that Ellen is in a better place with our
beloved Lord,
and I feel more comforted and hopeful
because the day will come when we all will be
together again with our Lord.

I will.
Thinking of Ellen
who we will meet in heaven soon.
Looking at the day.

We will
pray that you will overcome the evil one
in Thailand with Jesus our Lord.

I will pray that the sacrifice and love of the
missionaries
who lost their children and their wives in the land
of Joseon

in order to give us the Gospel, will not be in vain.

May each one perseveres and not give up
So that our efforts will not be in vain
but be used to further the Kingdom.

Missions cannot be done with modest commitment
but must exhibit a wholehearted dedication.
It is a spiritual battle.

We can't pray frivolously,
we have to be willing to stake our life
in order to save a soul.

Thinking of Ellen,
I think I can now pray willing to sacrifice my life.

Two missionaries,
When the Lord returns,
He will bring Ellen with Him,
While waiting for His return,
let us pray and prepare together for His return.

Every year at the end of May, Grace International School has an assembly where songs and music that the band and choir practiced throughout the year are presented. Tim Cocking, the choir director, wrote and composed a memorial song for Ellen after her death. When the song was presented at the school concert, the choir team sang together, commemorating Ellen.

All Stands Still

In memory of Ellen Her

Sometime we bend, sometime we break
We harvest what we did not sow
We all are fragile in the end
And made of dust, to dust I'll go
So many things were left unsaid:
How you were strong and you were brave
Now all I want is one more song
A little while to hear you play
In the quiet of your eyes,
all stands still

The stillness of your face, nothing will move
All of time flows through each day
But you are young and cannot die
I huddle in this little space
I turn my head and look away
The whisper of your voice,
all stands still

The stillness of your face, nothing will move
When will we see the light once more
When dark has turned,
When tears are dry
Sometimes break but sometimes bend,
Pieced back together again
In the stillness of this space

All stands still

Ellen has left us and is not with us anymore. However, it is not easy to overcome the pain. We still have to live our lives and everything around us is bustling, but we have to overcome this difficulty and time of pain in another given space. For a while it seems like we are moving around in our busy lives for a while, but time will slowly flow and in the meantime, these pains will be overcome. I want to overcome this difficult time. I write this song in remembrance of beloved Ellen who has already left. As I get older, I realize that our journey of life is will soon reach its end.

Now I think of Ellen in heaven with calmness and serenity. When our tears cease and darkness changes and into light, our lives will be renewed and we will also experience a beautiful, calm peace. Although Ellen is not here on earth right now, we share this song with a heartfelt desire that in heaven Ellen will hear this song sung again.

I leave a poem for Ellen who came to this land at an early age and was called to heaven.

A tiny seed is planted in this land
So small that it cannot be seen
It came like it wasn't even here
The Lord accepts her as a light for saving lives

The Lord of life called her
She traveled to heaven with the angels
Met Jesus' love and even saw hell
The Lord accepts her as a light for saving lives

She came with the gospel to a barren land
Her life to share heavenly life was given
In a dark land, but now it is lit for life
The Lord accepts her as a light for saving lives

Now, as a seed is buried here
The seed grew and brought other life
Life to life filled with abundant
The Lord accepts her as a light for saving lives

8. Until We See You Again

After finishing the funeral of our beloved Ellen, we retrieved Ellen's belongings from the dormitory of Grace International School in Chiang Mai.

Among her things, we came across a notebook written in Ellen's handwriting. There were a lot of words in the notes that said,

"I love you."

When Ellen was about four, five years old, she walked with her grandmother in New York. Her grandmother saw flowers and commented,

"This flower is so pretty!"

Then Ellen asked,

"Grandma! How about me? Grandma! Am I pretty, or is this flower pretty?".

Not only by her grandmother but by everyone in the family, she was loved.

She gradually began to say,

"I love you."

to others.

She was a child who enjoyed being loved and hugged. That's why she often expressed her love for others.

She was a child who would smile brightly when she heard others tell her,

"I love you."

She left us and is with the Lord to whom she wanted to return. I miss her so much. Whenever we see traces of Ellen, we are sad and tears flow freely. But we cannot continue being sad.

As the Lord has revealed to us, I believe that He planted Ellen as the seed for the thousands of souls who are dying, ignorant of Jesus in Thailand.

I hope that our remaining time on earth will be to serve the people of Thailand with passion as we share the Gospel of Jesus Christ. I do not want to be ashamed when I get to heaven to see Jesus and Ellen.

Epilogue

Epilogue

Index of Scriptural References

About the Author

Ellen Her Foundation

Epilogue

For several years, we did not know that Ellen had this wonderful spiritual experience when she was nine years old, and I did not listen to her during my church ministry in America. Ellen seems to have never thought that this spiritual experience as such a great event as to boast about it or that it was a very special experience given only to her. It was because she thought it was part of a regular Christians experience, so she did not tell anyone in our family. We only started hearing about it after the whole family went to Thailand as missionaries. It came out through our devotions each morning and in talking about experiences while sharing with each other.

At first, I was a bit skeptical, but when we heard the details of the heaven she had experienced, I found that a great deal of the details was already recorded in the Bible. The accounts were so specific and realistic that I could not just ignore what Ellen share. Of course I do not think that the images of heaven and hell that Ellen has seen are 100% accurate. Moreover, I admit that the details cannot all be verified by the Bible.

No one in this world could describe all of heaven perfectly except Jesus, the Lord of heaven. It may also be difficult to prove theologically the numerous details about heaven, which she has described. It may also be very different from other's experience of heaven and hell. It should be clear that this book is not for debate or argument about heaven.

Although much of what Ellen has seen is a very tiny fragment of heaven, I hope that it will be used to help all those who believe in Jesus to long for the heaven to come. As I prayed, I realized that the Lord wanted me to share Ellen's experience of heaven with others. Many people think too lightly about heaven and hell and therefore do not see the importance of paying attention to these eternal destinations. It is my hope that they would realize that only through Jesus can they avoid hell and find a home in heaven.

I am thankful if this heavenly testimony could have a small benefit to the community of faith who live with expectation regarding the Kingdom of Heaven and of the promise of Jesus to come back soon.

I would also be truly grateful if one or two of those who read this testimony would come to Jesus and realize the concrete reality of heaven and hell.

Although we are missionaries serving the souls of Thailand with the gospel of Jesus Christ, the wonderful experience of heaven and hell that Ellen described renewed our calling.

As missionaries, we are convinced that this is a crucial truth that must be told not only for casual interest, but to say to the many souls of the land of Thailand that heaven surely exists.

If you are a Christian who is reading this book, we hope you will be able to convey the existence of heaven and hell convincingly to the people around you who are walking toward hell without Jesus Christ.

That is the purpose and reason for our Christian presence in this world.

After sharing the testimony of her experiences of heaven and hell, our family had to move to another area in Thailand. After being home-schooled for about two and a half years in the rural areas, Ellen went to the dormitory and studied at the Grace International School, a school for missionaries' kids, about five and a half hours away from the place where we were ministering. She entered as an 8th grade. After finishing one semester of 8th grade there, one week prior to her 14th birthday, she entered into the arms of Jesus, whom she loved so much and wanted to see again ahead of her mom and dad.

At the age of nine,
the Lord called Ellen to show her heaven and hell
and then took her to be with Him.
A child who always laughed brightly and clearly.
A child who always shared her happy smile to others

And spread a Happy Virus.

A child who was always full of lively energy.

A child who loved to dance so much.

While remembering the beautiful and precious devotion of the first missionary in Thailand-one of the many Ellen saw in heaven-we laid her body to rest in the land of Thailand at Tak.

Now she has become the seed of the Kingdom of God for Thailand.

I pray that this little testimony will be used in to make heaven and hell real and to make Jesus more approachable, so that Ellen's death may not be in vain. Her passing away at such a young age brought sorrow to those who loved her, but her legacy will bring life to many.

Ellen is no longer in this world, but I leave this book in commemoration of my beloved child.

The Lord said,

"Surely I will come quickly."

"Amen. Even so, Come, Lord Jesus."

Bible verses about the Heaven and Hell

God and the saints

1 John 1:5 God is light; in him there is no darkness at all.

James 1:17 Every good and perfect gift is from above, coming down from the Father of the heavenly lights, who does not change like shifting shadows.

1 Thessalonians 5:5 For you are all children of light, children of the day. We are not of the night or of the darkness.

Luke 16:8 The master commended the dishonest manager for his shrewdness. For the sons of this world are more shrewd in dealing with their own generation than the sons of light.

John 12:36 While you have the light, believe in the light, that you may become sons of light.

Isaiah 60:19 The sun will no more be your light by day, nor will the brightness of the moon shine on you, for the LORD will be your everlasting light, and your God will be your glory.

Jesus Christ

Revelation 1:13-16 And among the lampstands was someone like a son of man, dressed in a robe reaching down to his feet and with a golden sash around his chest. The hair on his head was white like wool, as white as snow, and his eyes were like blazing fire.

His feet were like bronze glowing in a furnace, and his voice was like the sound of rushing waters.

In his right hand he held seven stars, and coming out of his mouth was a sharp, double-edged sword. His face was like the sun shining in all its brilliance.

Revelation 1 :18 I am the Living One; I was dead, and now look, I am alive for ever and ever! And I hold the keys of death and Hades.

Revelation 19:12-13 His eyes are like blazing fire, and on his head are many crowns. He has a name written on him that no one knows but he himself. He is dressed in a robe dipped in blood, and his name is the Word of God.

Revelation 22 :13 I am the Alpha and the Omega, the First and the Last, the Beginning and the End.

Revelation 22:20 He who testifies to these things says, "Yes, I am coming soon." Amen. Come, Lord Jesus.

Heaven

Matthew 17:2 His clothes became white as light.

Matthew 25:34 Then the King will say to those on his right, 'Come, you who are blessed by my Father, inherit the kingdom prepared for you from the foundation of the world.

Matthew 26:64 Jesus said to him, "You have said so. But I tell you, from now on you will see the Son of Man seated at the right hand of Power and coming on the clouds of heaven."

Mark 10:15 Truly, I say to you, whoever does not receive the kingdom of God like a child shall not enter it.

Mark 10:24-25 Jesus said to them again, "Children, how difficult it is to enter the kingdom of God! It is easier for a camel to go through the eye of a needle than for a rich person to enter the kingdom of God."

Mark 9:3 His clothes became radiant, intensely white, as no one on earth could bleach them.

Mark 10:29-30 "Truly, I say to you, there is no one who has left house or brothers or sisters or mother or father or children or lands, for my sake and for the gospel, who will not receive a hundredfold now in this time, houses and brothers and sisters and mothers and children and lands, with persecutions, and in the age to come eternal life.

Revelation 2:7 To the one who is victorious, I will give the right to eat from the tree of life, which is in the paradise of God.

Revelation 2:10 Be faithful, even to the point of death, and I will give you life as your victor's crown

Revelation 3:5 The one who is victorious will, like them, be dressed in white. I will never blot out the name of that person from the book of life, but will acknowledge that name before my Father and his angels

Revelation 3:20 Here I am! I stand at the door and knock. If anyone hears my voice and opens the door, I will come in and eat with that person, and they with me

Revelation 4: 2-3 There before me was a throne in heaven with someone sitting on it. And the one who sat there had the appearance of jasper and ruby. A rainbow that shone like an emerald encircled the throne.

Revelation 4:4 They were dressed in white and had crowns of gold on their heads

Revelation 4:6 In front of the throne there was what looked like a sea of glass, clear as crystal.

Revelation 21:1-2 Then I saw "a new heaven and a new earth," for the first heaven and the first earth had passed away, and there was no longer any sea. I saw the Holy City, the new Jerusalem, coming down out of heaven from God, prepared as a bride beautifully dressed for her husband.

Revelation 21:11-12 It shone with the glory of God, and its brilliance was like that of a very precious jewel, like a jasper, clear as crystal. It had a great, high wall with twelve gates, and with twelve angels at the gates. On the gates were written the names of the twelve tribes of Israel.

Revelation 21:21 The great street of the city was of gold, as pure as transparent glass

Revelation 21:23 The city does not need the sun or the moon to shine on it, for the glory of God gives it light, and the Lamb is its lamp.

Revelation 21:27 Nothing impure will ever enter it, nor will anyone who does what is shameful or deceitful, but only those whose names are written in the Lamb's book of life.

Revelation 21:25 On no day will its gates ever be shut, for there will be no night there.

Revelation 22:1-2 Then the angel showed me the river of the water of life, as clear as crystal, flowing from the throne of God and of the Lamb down the middle of the great street of the city. On each side of the river stood the tree of life, bearing twelve crops of fruit, yielding its fruit every month. And the leaves of the tree are for the healing of the nations.

Revelation 22:5 There will be no more night. They will not need the light of a lamp or the light of the sun, for the Lord God will give them light. And they will reign for ever and ever.

Revelation 22:7 "Look, I am coming soon! Blessed is the one who keeps the words of the prophecy written in this scroll."

Revelation 22:12 "Look, I am coming soon! My reward is with me, and I will give to each person according to what they have done."

Angel

Matthew 18:10 I tell you that in heaven their angels always see the face of my Father who is in heaven.

Matthew 26:53 Do you think that I cannot appeal to my Father, and he will at once send me more than twelve legions of angels?

Mark 12:25 For when they rise from the dead, they neither marry nor are given in marriage, but are like angels in heaven.

Hebrew 1: 14 Are not all angels ministering spirits sent to serve those who will inherit salvation?

Revelation 5:11 Then I looked and heard the voice of many angels, numbering thousands upon thousands, and ten thousand times ten thousand.

Matthew 22:30 For in the resurrection they neither marry nor are given in marriage, but are like angels in heaven.

Mark 12:25 For when they rise from the dead, they neither marry nor are given in marriage, but are like angels in heaven.

Life in Heaven

Revelation 5:9 And they sang a new song, saying: "You are worthy to take the scroll and to open its seals, because you were slain, and with your blood you purchased for God persons from every tribe and language and people and nation.

Revelation 7:9 here before me was a great multitude that no one could count, from every nation, tribe, people and language, standing before the throne and before the Lamb. They were wearing white robes and were holding palm branches in their hands.

Revelation 7:15 Therefore, "they are before the throne of God and serve him day and night in his temple; and he who sits on the throne will shelter them with his presence.

Revelation 7: 17 For the Lamb at the center of the throne will be their shepherd; 'he will lead them to springs of living water.' 'And God will wipe away every tear from their eyes.'"

Revelation 19:7-8 Let us rejoice and be glad and give him glory! For the wedding of the Lamb has come, and his bride has made herself ready. Fine linen, bright and clean, was given her to wear." (Fine linen stands for the righteous acts of God's holy people.)

Revelation 20:4 They had not worshiped the beast or its image and had not received its mark on their foreheads or their hands. They came to life and reigned with Christ a thousand years.

Revelation 20:12 And I saw the dead, great and small, standing before the throne, and books were opened. Another book was opened, which is the book of life. The dead were judged according to what they had done as recorded in the books.

Revelation 21:4 'He will wipe every tear from their eyes. There will be no more death' or mourning or crying or pain, for the old order of things has passed away."

Isaiah 65:24-25 Before they call I will answer; while

they are still speaking I will hear. The wolf and the lamb will feed together, and the lion will eat straw like the ox, and dust will be the serpent's food. They will neither harm nor destroy on all my holy mountain," says the LORD.

Hell

Matthew 18:8-9 And if your hand or your foot causes you to sin, cut it off and throw it away. It is better for you to enter life crippled or lame than with two hands or two feet to be thrown into the eternal fire. And if your eye causes you to sin, tear it out and throw it away. It is better for you to enter life with one eye than with two eyes to be thrown into the hell of fire.

Mark 9:48-49 'where their worm does not die and the fire is not quenched.' For everyone will be salted with fire.

Matt 22:13 'Bind him hand and foot and cast him into the outer darkness. In that place there will be weeping and gnashing of teeth.'

Matt 25:30 And cast the worthless servant into the outer darkness. In that place there will be weeping and gnashing of teeth.'

Matt 25:41 "Then he will say to those on his left, 'Depart from me, you cursed, into the eternal fire prepared for the devil and his angels.

2 Peter 2:17 These people are springs without water and mists driven by a storm. Blackest darkness is reserved for them

Jude 1:6 And the angels who did not keep their positions of authority but abandoned their proper dwelling—these he has kept in darkness, bound with everlasting chains for judgment on the great Day.

Revelation 14:10-11 They, too, will drink the wine of God's fury, which has been poured full strength into the cup of his wrath. They will be tormented with burning sulfur in the presence of the holy angels and of the Lamb. And the smoke of their torment will rise for ever and ever. There will be no rest day or night for those who worship the beast and its image, or for anyone who receives the mark of its name

Revelation 20:14-15 Then death and Hades were thrown into the lake of fire. The lake of fire is the second death. Anyone whose name was not found written in the book of life was thrown into the lake of fire

Devil, Evil spirit

Matthew 12:43-44 When an impure spirit comes out of a person, it goes through arid places seeking rest and does not find it. Then it says, 'I will return to the house I left.' When it arrives, it finds the house unoccupied, swept clean and put in order.

Mark 3:11 whenever the unclean spirits saw him, they fell down before him and cried out, "You are the Son of God."

Mark 3:22 And the scribes who came down from Jerusalem were saying, "He is possessed by Beelzebul," and "by the prince of demons he casts out the demons."

Mark 3:30, 5:2, 6:7, 7:25, 9:25
"He has an unclean spirit."

2 Peter 2:4-5 For if God did not spare angels when they sinned, but sent them to hell, putting them in chains of darkness to be held for judgment

Revelation 12:9 The great dragon was hurled down-that ancient serpent called the devil, or Satan, who leads the whole world astray. He was hurled to the earth, and his angels with him.

Revelation 20:2 He seized the dragon, that ancient serpent, who is the devil, or Satan, and bound him for a thousand years.

Zechariah 13:2 "On that day, I will banish the names of the idols from the land, and they will be remembered no more," declares the LORD Almighty. "I will remove both the prophets and the spirit of impurity from the land.

Paul's experience and desires

2 Corinthian 12:2-3 I know a man in Christ who fourteen years ago was caught up to the third heaven--whether in the body or out of the body I do not know, God knows.
And I know that this man was caught up into paradise--whether in the body or out of the body I do not know, God knows...

Philippians 1:23-24 I am hard pressed between the two. My desire is to depart and be with Christ, for that is far better. But to remain in the flesh is more necessary on your account.

About Author

Soosung Her

Missionary Soosung Her, was discipled through the organization, Disciple of Christ Fellowship (DCF) and served with them for more than 10 years. He graduated from Chong- Shin University Seminary in Korea and was ordained as a minister. He served in churches both in Korea and the USA. He was called as a missionary while serving in a church in the USA. As a missionary of WEC International in Thailand, he is serving the unreached people in the Central North region through church planting and through raising up leaders for the next generation. He is serving in this country with his wife Ihnyoung, and they have raised two daughters. Rin is studying at a university in USA and Ellen Eun at the age of thirteen was laid to rest in the Tak region of Thailand as the seed of the Kingdom of God for Thailand.

Ellen Eun Her

Ellen was born in New York City, USA and she was grown up there until ten years of age.

When Ellen was nine years old she attended a retreat named Ecclesia in Promise church where she experienced heaven and hell.

At the age of ten she moved to Thailand as a missionary kid when she was only in fifth grade with her family.

She now lays peacefully in the Tak province located in central north of Thailand

as a seed of the Kingdom of God for Thailand.

After she passed away, Ellen Her Foundation was established in USA, South Korea and Thailand to commemorate her.

Ellen Her Foundation

Ellen Her Foundation has been established in 2018 to commemorate Ellen Her, who became a seed of the Kingdom of God for Thailand.

This foundation focuses on the evangelism for Thailand.

Our mission is

1. to establish a Christian school.

2. to award scholarships for Thai students.

3. to make disciples of the Thai youth.

4. to church planting.

5. to publish the Christian books.

We need,

Teachers : English Science Math Korean
Music   Computer Counselor
Physical Education etc.

Volunteers : Culture, Food and Constructor

Contact Us:

    35 Sparrowhawk Irvine, CA 92604

    Tel 718 509 9078 / 949 351 5020 (in USA)

        66 082 808 2015 (in Thailand)

    E-mail : tccofhs@gmail.com

    Kakao Talk ID : Heaven2000